A
PHILOSOPHY
OF THE
SECOND
ADVENT

A
PHILOSOPHY
OF THE
SECOND
ADVENT

Howard A. Redmond

MOTT
MEDIA

A PHILOSOPHY OF THE SECOND ADVENT

First Edition

Designed and edited by Leonard George Goss
Typeset by Joyce Bohn

Manufactured in the United States of America
ISBN 0-88062-067-6

**This book is dedicated to the
memory of my mother
Ada M. Redmond (1905-1980),
one of the saints who will "rise first"
(1 Thess. 4:16)**

FOREWORD

The second coming of Jesus Christ is a cardinal doctrine of the Christian faith. From that moment when Jesus was taken up into a cloud while his disciples stood by amazed and two men appeared, dressed in white, saying, "This very Jesus who has been taken up from you into Heaven will come back in just the same way as you have seen him go" (Acts 1:11, Phillips), the believing church has taken as part of its basic credo the truth that Christ will return to this earth in point of time to bring to completion the redemptive program of God for man.

The doctrine has been abused. Some, like the Montanists, have read into the Return a literalism never intended. Others, embarrassed by any theistic intrusion into the natural order, have allegorized the promised return into a poetic expression of well-intentioned human aspirations. (Someone noted that whenever the church has been divided on a basic issue the truth falls somewhere in between. Eschatology is no exception!)

Howard Redmond is a balanced exegete and philosopher. He distinguishes with care between the extremes in eschatological teaching. For instance, while recognizing that in one sense Christ "comes" in the gift to the early church of the Holy Spirit, there nevertheless will be a final historical reappearance of Jesus on earth. While we cannot know the exact time of his coming we can know with certainty that he will come.

In a time when so many popular speakers talk about finding in today's newspaper the fulfillment of specific prophecies from both the Old and New Testament, it is refreshing to read

an extended essay by a scholar who has a proper understanding of the nature of prophetic literature and doesn't lose sight of the forest in his examination of the trees. You will enjoy the irenic spirit of the author, his familiarity with literature and philosophy, and his penchant for the well-turned phrase.

For the layman *A Philosophy of the Second Advent* will throw into bold relief a central doctrine of New Testament theology. It will quicken the pulse of all those who by faith have entered into a saving relationship with the One who will most certainly return. History, Redmond points out, is not cyclical: it is heading toward a specific goal. The return of Christ is that *telos*—that goal which brings into focus God's plan to reconcile to himself all who in faith will surrender to his love.

Robert H. Mounce

PREFACE

"What—another book about the Second Coming?" The author will not think harshly of any reader who so greets this book. For in the sixties and seventies there has indeed been a plethora of books about the return of Christ. To some this fact has meant the moving of God's Spirit in preparation for the "end time." To those of opposite disposition, it may indicate the extent of human credulity. But whatever evaluation may be given, it is an undeniable bibliographical fact that numerous recent books on the subject are available.

Why another one, then? Several reasons suggest themselves. One is the poor quality and, at times, sensationalism of much of the recent output. Typical books on the subject are often written by someone representing a narrow point of view with some special theological axe to grind, often of limited educational background and of inadequate knowledge and appreciation of the history of the church. In a word, they are sectarian. They stand at the street corners of the mind, passing out their tracts; but in this case books, not tracts are distributed—and they are not free!

This book, on the contrary, attempts to build upon the foundation of both faith *and* reason, Jerusalem *and* Athens, Wittenberg-Geneva *and* Oxford-Cambridge, Reformation *and* Renaissance. If there can be any uniqueness to a book about the return of Christ in an age surfeited with this theme, it is the claim that this book shows the rationality of this belief. In addition to presenting a discussion of the Second Coming that is true to the Bible and the best of reason and of church history, a major purpose of this writing is to show the subject as a vital part of Christian philosophy, especially the philosophy of history. The book may fairly be judged by its success or failure to fulfill this intention.

Another reason for the making of the book is the conviction that the Bible, enlightened Christian understanding and world events conspire to make this study an intellectual necessity. "World events?" one may ask. Yes, for though the book does not state the latest figures from the stock exchange or the most recent statistics on Russian weaponry foreshadowed in the Book of Revelation, it does not ignore current events. Since Jesus himself spoke of the "signs of the times," they should not be ignored. Obviously, Jesus' statement, "When you see these things, lift up your heads!" was not the advice of a physical therapist recommending neck exercises!

Since there is such a variety of positions on this issue, the reader may ask at the outset, "Where does the author stand?" Reared among ardent premillennialists, I came to reject that position because of its many excesses. But even in the rejection I retain a certain sympathy for the faith it represents. My feeling toward it is similar to that I felt for our old car. Though it needed many repairs, it was not yet ready for the dump. Though the external package I came to know as extreme premillennialism may deserve to be consigned to the scrapheap, inside that package was something I did not wish to lose.

It is that treasure-within-the-package that I am endeavoring to uncover and preserve in this book. The result will not

match any one of the traditional millennial positions. For the three classical millennarian views I see as large ruts impeding the progress of Christian thought, though each school undoubtedly makes important contributions to the whole of Christian truth. I hope these pages may present the New Testament view of Christ's return, uncluttered by millennarian or other accretions, and yet take full account of the best of biblical scholarship (Such writers as Reinhold Niebuhr, A. M. Hunter, T. F. Torrance, and G. B. Caird are among my mentors in this area).

Perhaps a word needs to be said about the dating of New Testament books. There has been a general or "consensus" dating of many books that is common to most of the world's theological scholarship, American and European. However, conservative scholars sometimes disagree with the commonly accepted dating, almost always on the earlier side. In general I have followed the consensus dating, but in cases where the time of writing becomes especially important (e.g. the Pastoral Epistles, and particularly 2 Peter), note will be made of the differences in dating. It is interesting that Bishop John Robinsons's recent book, *Redating the New Testament*, though by one commonly perceived as a liberal, supports early dates usually favored by conservatives.

In the midst of a busy teaching schedule it is tempting to put off the completion of book writing. With most other books this may be legitimate. But in the writing process I was impressed with a sense of urgency. If C. S. Lewis is right that our duty is to be ready for the anytime coming of Christ, I cannot resist the feeling that this book should be read while it is still needed and may do some good—or to put it bluntly, that a book about Christ's return should appear before he returns! It is with the prayer that these pages may help people be ready for his coming that I write these words now. "Come, Lord Jesus" (Rev. 22:20).

Finally, I want to thank those who aided me in the preparation of this manuscript. First, my gratitude to Whitworth College for the sabbatical leave that started my research, and to the members of the Religion Department, especially Dr. Roger Mohrlang, with whom I had penetrating conversations over many a cup of tea. Nor would I forget our fine student secretary, Melissa Norton, who spent long hours typing the manuscript, and in general—perhaps inspired by Genesis 1—brought order out of chaos. I also express my thanks to student Douglas McCleary for help on the "end-time" section of the Appendix; to Prof. Siegfried Risse, of Essen, West Germany, for most helpful suggestions regarding this book's title; and to the library staff of Moody Bible Institute for the Moody sermon in the Appendix. I also acknowledge my indebtedness to the Presbyterian Board of Christian Education and its *Enquirer Magazine*, Sept.-Nov., 1968 for helpful material used in Chapter 8. And my special thanks to my wife Lois and our children Colleen and Calvin, who encouraged me at many points; and to the host of Christians I have met over the years who have given me inspiration as they have "loved his appearing."

CONTENTS

Foreword by Robert H. Mounce vii

Preface... ix

Part I *He Will Certainly Return*

Chapter 1   Old Testament Evidence for the
Second Coming...................... 3

Chapter 2   New Testament Evidence
of Christ's Return 11

Paul's Message: Work and Wait

The Synoptic Gospels and Christ's Return

    Mark: A Message of Expectancy
    Matthew: A Message of Faithfulness
    Luke & Acts: A Message of Caution

The General Letters

    Hebrews: Eagerly Waiting
    James: Patience in Waiting
    1 Peter: Preparation for Christ's Return
    The Letters of John: Comfort While Waiting
    2 Peter: Assurance of Christ's Return

Revelation: Hope in Suffering

In Summary

Part II *The Time of His Return*

Chapter 3   Comfort and Caution 47

What About Date Setting?
What About Signs of Christ's Coming?

Chapter 4   What About the Millennium? 57

What Is Premillennialism?
What Is Postmillennialism?
What Is Amillennialism?
What About the Antichrist?

In Summary

Chapter 5   The Church and the Second Coming:
             Cults and Neglect 63

             Montanism
             Neglect of the Second Coming
             Anabaptists
             Seventh Day Adventists and Jehovah's Witnesses
             Recent Cults
             Why Heresies?

Part III   *Therefore, We Must Always be Ready for Him*

Chapter 6   How Does the Second Coming
             Affect Me? 73

             Spiritual Readiness

                 Personal Salvation
                 Right Living
                 Motivation for Evangelism
                 Worship
                 Creeds and Confessions
                 Motivation to Serve

Chapter 7   Why is the Philosophy of Christ's
             Return Important? 83

             Intellectual Preparation

                 Epistemology
                 Ethics
                 Logic
                 Philosophy of History
                     Aristotle
                     John Scotus Erigena
                     Pierre Tielhard de Chardin
                     Emil Brunner

             How Does the Philosophy of Christ's Return
             Affect the World?

                 Evolution and the Return of Christ

             Other Philosophies of the Second Coming

             What Does It matter?

Chapter 8   The Ultimate Liberation 101

Epilogue: The Once and Future King............ 105

Appendix:

Sectarian Understandings
    of the Return 119

"End-Time" Writers 121

The Author's Choices 127

C. S. Lewis 131

Preface to Moody Sermon 135

"The Second Coming of Christ,"
    by D. L. Moody.................. 137

Notes 149

Bibliography 151

Part One

"He will certainly return"

—C. S. Lewis, *The World's Last Night*

CHAPTER 1

Old Testament Evidence for the Second Coming

The early Christians were in the mainstream of Middle Eastern culture. They did not live in a cultural or religious vacuum. Their religious parentage was obviously that set of beliefs and practices we know as Judaism, embracing both the Old Testament itself and the body of commentary and tradition that had grown around it. Their belief in the return of Christ was to be explained not only by the teaching of Christ, but by that teaching as understood in the context of Judaism (Jesus, of course, spoke from that same context). In that light, the Old Testament background becomes of critical importance, for it surely determined the form and to some extent the content of their belief in His coming again.

Probably no Old Testament idea is more basic to early Christian belief in the return than the Day of the Lord. Originally this was a doctrine of a golden age for Israel when her enemies would be subdued and she would rise to unparalleled heights of glory. The prophets (Isaiah 9:2; 11:1; Jeremiah 23:5; Ezekiel 34:23) and psalmists, among others (Ps. 72), tell of such a day characterized by prosperity and peace.

After the division of the kingdom in 922 B.C., these expectations were entertained in the Northern Kingdom during the reign of Jeroboam II (786-46 B.C.), when Israel enjoyed economic affluence and surcease from war. The people felt sure God's kingdom was just around the corner; the Day of the Lord, understood as a time of exaltation for Israel, was almost upon them.

It caused more than a mild shock, then, when the prophet Amos came upon the scene thundering:

> Woe to you who desire the day of the Lord . . .
> It is darkness and not light . . .
> and gloom with no brightness in it.
>
> (Amos 5:18,20)

Denouncing the people for their national and personal sins, Amos ultimately saw no hope. They were crooked like a badly built wall (7:7-8); They were rotten like a bowl of overripe fruit (8:1-2). An idea that in some other Old Testament writers had a positive and almost euphoric connotation becomes in Amos a cause for lament. For Israel, the Day of the Lord *was* coming soon; but sadly it would be a day of disaster.

Later prophets followed Amos in their understanding of the Day of the Lord. In Zephaniah (630-621 B.C.) it is the *dies irae*, the day of wrath and judgment upon Israel as well as the world.

> "The great day of the Lord is near, it is near and hastening fast . . . A day of wrath is that day, a day of distress and anguish, a day or ruin and devastation, a day of darkness and gloom, a day of clouds and thick darkness"
>
> (Zeph. 1:14-15).

The prophet Joel (400-350 B.C.) saw a plague of locusts as a symbol of the day of the Lord: "Alas for the day! For the day of the Lord is near, and as destruction from the Almighty it comes" (Joel 1:15). But he goes further than earlier prophets to see beyond the judgments: "It shall come to pass

afterward, that I will pour out my spirit on all flesh . . . And it shall come to pass that all who call upon the name of the Lord shall be delivered" (Joel 2:28,32). In a later section of Isaiah (25:9) and in Daniel (7:10) judgment is seen as followed by divine graciousness and rule.

It is not difficult to see how Christians would relate Jesus' teaching about his coming again to what they had already learned in Judaism. To them, it was an updating of what they had known before: That God would one day come in judgment, which would be followed by peace and rebuilding. William Barclay states unequivocally: "To the Christian the Second Coming of Jesus Christ was indeed the Day of the Lord."[1]

Further comment should be made concerning another aspect of the Old Testament background, apocalyptic literature. This is a special literary genre that presents its message mainly in symbolism. Usually arising in a time of national crisis, it sees reality in a dualistic, black-white way and views the divine kingdom as coming suddenly, even violently, like a bolt out of the blue. The best known biblical examples are the books of Daniel (in part) and Revelation. Coming out of the period between the Old and New Testaments were other apocalyptic books, which form a part of the Apocrypha. Such apocalytic writing was probably not a major influence on the New Testament's view of the return. Its main contribution seems to have been in the area of *form*, that is, the way in which the New Testament belief was stated (For example, the form of Paul's teaching about the return of 1 Thessalonians 4—including trumpet-blowing and archangel's call—is regarded by many scholars as derived from Jewish apocalyptic; but this is not to say that the substance of Paul's message is thus derived). But I see no solid evidence that the essential content of the New Testament belief is apocalyptically rooted. To say that Christian belief in the return came mainly from apocalyptic would be to put it under a cloud, for apocalypticism, while

a part of the Bible, is usually regarded as secondary. It is my thesis that the Christian belief is rooted in the Old Testament as a whole, including the law and particularly the prophets, with apocalypticism a minor although significant part of the whole.

Other Old Testament emphases also contribute to the idea of the return. One is implicit in the concept of the Messiah. Christians see the basic messianic promises fulfilled in the life, death and resurrection of Jesus of Nazareth. But not all the Old Testament promises have yet been realized. Only in the return shall we find their complete fulfillment. As H. H. Rowley puts it, though to us there is a long interval between the First and Second Comings, "to prophets who saw the future afar off, the depth in time was lost as depth in space is lost to the eye of one who looks at the stars, and the First and Second Advent are therefore fused in prophecy."[2]

Isaiah 9:2-7 is a good example. Many Old Testament scholars assume that this was originally a poem to celebrate the ascension of a king in Jerusalem. It culminates in the famous verses:

> For to us a child is born, to us a son is given;
> and the government will be upon his shoulder,
> And his name will be called
> Wonderful Counselor, Mighty God,
> Everlasting Father, Prince of Peace.
> Of the increase of his government and of peace
> There will be no end.
>
> (Isaiah 9:6,7)

Surely a Christian sees in these verses much that reminds him of Jesus, not the least of which is the Christmas-like theme of the birth of a child. But how fully can we say this passage—regarded by most Christians as messianic—applies to the first coming of Christ? Was the government upon His shoulder? Was He "in battle god-like" (The New English Bible translation of "Mighty God")? In what sense was He the Prince of

Peace? Or is this title more appropriate to His Second Coming? We need not at the moment try to answer these questions, but may see in them an illustration of Rowley's point that "the First and Second Advent are . . . fused in prophecy." The first coming by itself does not complete these promises, though surely we can perceive the beginning of their realization in Jesus of Nazareth.

A special aspect of Jesus as Messiah is His place as ultimate occupant of the throne of David. Beginning in 2 Samuel 7, with Nathan's promise to David that "your house and your kingdom shall be made sure forever before me; your throne shall be established forever," the "line of David" runs through the Old Testament and into the New, culminating in the New Testament's opening words, "Jesus Christ, the Son of David." Prophets warned kings that to follow a wrong course of action would be to cut themselves out of David's lineage: "If you do not believe," Isaiah warned young King Ahaz, "surely you will not be established" (Isaiah 7:9). The writer of Psalm 89, building on 2 Samuel 7, glories in the promises to David and restates them in powerful language: "His line shall endure forever, his throne as long as the sun before me. Like the moon it shall be established forever; it shall stand firm while the skies endure" (Ps. 89:36-37). Granting what to Western ears is the seemingly extravagant language common to the Middle East, it is difficult to see these words being realized in the reign of a king ruling a Rhode Island-sized nation from the area of a few square blocks that was Old Testament Jerusalem. G. von Rad suggests that some Israelites may have had doubts about such strong language applying to each Israelite king, and may have asked "Art thou he who is come, or shall we look for another?"

A comment should be made about the nature of Old Testament prophecy. Many Bible-believing Christians have been brought up to believe that Isaiah (Isa. 7:14; 9:6-7), Micah (Micah 5:2) and others who talked about a coming deliverer

were knowingly and directly speaking specifically of Jesus of Nazareth, as if history were being written ahead of time. The liberal reaction to that view would say the prophets were talking *only* about people in or near their own time, and that the prophecies have nothing to do with Jesus. I must speak my deep conviction that the truth is between the extremes. Doubtless Isaiah did have an imminent birth in mind when he said in Isaiah 7:14, "A young women shall conceive and bear a son" (indeed, the translation of the Jerusalem Bible, "A young woman has conceived . . ." would underscore even more the imminence of the birth!). Probably the Isaiah 9 passage culminating in the famous words, "Unto us a child is born," was written to celebrate the ascension of a Hebrew king. The "suffering servant" passages of Isaiah 40-55 may have been written originally about an individual in recent or distant Hebrew history. And certain "messianic Psalms" were likely written about the splendor of Hebrew kings (Psalms 2, 110). But all these passages are seen by Christians as messianic in the sense that no mere human being could ever satisfy them; there is a "plus" to the prophecies that are fully realized only in Jesus (the New Testament explicitly claims most of the above prophecies as messianic and pointing to Jesus). G. A. Smith beautifully illustrates this by observing that tidal rivers are themselves affected by the sea into which they flow.[3] So the Old Testament prophecies flow into the sea of Christ, but are themselves affected by that into which they run. The prophecies, then, have a larger meaning than they did when written. In the Old Testament there was an *immediate* fulfillment of the prophecy (such as the birth of a child within a year of Isaiah's statement in 7:14), but the New Testament sees the *ultimate* fulfillment in Jesus of Nazareth.

All this well illustrates Augustine's point in his famous saying: "The New Testament is in the Old concealed, the Old is in the New revealed." The Old Testament provides substantial background for Christian belief in the return of Christ.

The full implication of Jesus as Messiah, including messianic reign and kingdom, was seen by early Christians as including both the First and Second Comings of Jesus. And the concept of the Day of the Lord easily became, for Christians, the Day of Christ (Phil. 2:16). Now let us look to the New Testament teaching on the coming again of our Lord.

CHAPTER 2

New Testament Evidence of Christ's Return

PAUL'S MESSAGE: WORK AND WAIT

The earliest of New Testament teachings on the return, and surely one of the most significant, is that of Paul. We shall therefore begin our survey of the New Testament doctrine with the thoughts of the great apostle, because of both their prominence and priority. Next, the gospels, which are later than Paul's letters, will be considered in the light of Paul's ideas.

Where did Paul receive his knowledge of the return? One answer might be, "in the Damascus Road experience." It is certainly true that Paul's life and ideas were dramatically changed by his conversion. In a sense, all that Paul was to do and speak for the rest of his life was determined at that moment. But it would be unwise to read into that experience specific knowledge of particular aspects of Christian theology. Paul was like a maiden who has just said "yes" to her suitor: She may not at that moment know many details of her future, except that it will be with her husband. "It would be a mistake," says James Stewart, "to suppose that the full

implications of his amazing experience were evident to the apostle from the first."[4] Paul had said "yes" to the divine Suitor; the rest would follow in time.

Another answer might be to say that Paul received his knowledge of the return during his retreat into the "Arabian desert" (Gal. 1:17). We know little of what happened during that very early post-conversion phase of Paul's Christian life. Paul himself may have regarded it as a time of direct revelation, for he says of his gospel, "I did not receive it from man, nor was I taught it, but by the revelation of Jesus Christ" (Gal. 1:12). Though Paul does not specifically say he received the revelation during his desert experience, it is tempting to assume that this is at least part of his meaning. In his well-known biography, Edgar Goodspeed, true to his liberalism, saw the desert in psychological terms, a time when Paul was able "to reconstruct his inner world." Surely both views could be true. But so little is said about the details of the event that it would be hazardous to say that Paul emerged from the desert with a complete theological agenda. Though his knowledge was surely more definite and advanced than after his conversion, we still cannot say that either or both of the experiences constituted the fountain of eschatological information.

What then, was the principal source of his knowledge of Christ's return? The answer I suggest may seem overly simple, but there is a noble philosophical tradition ("Occam's Razor") that the simplest explanation is the true one! Paul's knowledge of Christ's return is most adequately understood as derived from the common, shared expectation of the early Christian community, though we must not rule out unique or special revelation to Paul. Whereas unique revelation concerning the return *may* have been given to Paul, (and arguments from silence are always precarious), we are sure that Paul, as a prominent member of the early Christian community learned as he helped organize and refine its beliefs. Obviously, Paul reflected the belief of the earliest Christian community. If one

wishes to find what Christians believed in the middle of the First Century, much could be learned from the letters of Paul that were written at the time. He was both teacher and student. As Paul matured in the fellowship of believers, he also helped that fellowship focus and direct their beliefs. He who was taught by both the community and personal revelation in time became the teacher.

How prominent was the return to Paul's thinking? It was at the very heart of the body of doctrine we call Pauline. Modern interpreters of Paul have sometimes tried to "play down" this emphasis in his thought because it may not be congenial to the prevailing cultural assumptions. But we can no more excise this idea from Paul than we can eliminate the prince of Denmark from *Hamlet*. As an example, consider one of the most familiar verses in Paul's writing, the conclusion of the great "Love chapter," 1 Corinthians 13: "So faith, hope, love abide, these three; but the greatest of these is love." A good deal has been said of Paul's view of *faith* and *love* but what of *hope*? Is this simply a psychological goal, like the hope of recess or lunch to the school child sweating out an hour of arithmetic or spelling? Most students of Paul do not think so. They rather see it as *hope for the return of Christ*. If this view is correct, then, the return was not an ancillary or peripheral doctrine, but one indispensable to the faith as Paul understood it.

This does not mean that Paul always gave the same emphasis to the doctrine. Generally, the return was more explicit in earlier epistles than in the later. The doctrine may be prominent in one letter and recede in another, but as J. Stewart observes, "that does not mean it has been lost. Sooner or later it reappears."[5] It would be fair to say that as time passed, the whole of First Century Christianity, including Paul, gradually came to feel that the Christ's return had been "delayed" (see Matt. 25:5), and would not take place in their lifetime. But this is not to say that in any sense they abandoned the doctrine. While

it was central to their ethics and thinking, it was less obvious because other immediate concerns such as persecution, heresy, Christian-Jewish relations, and church organization also occupied their minds. Indeed, the fact that later writings refer to the doctrine less often and in less dramatic fashion may show the extent to which it had become completely basic to Christian thinking (we do not commonly speak of physical gravity in every other sentence, simply because it is so basic we need not talk about it often; though in Newton's day, when it was being definitively stated, it was talked about a great deal).

In summary, what was proclaimed *fortissimo* in Paul's earlier writings is still proclaimed in later books, but it is *mezzoforte*, and is often contrapuntal to other themes in the apostle's thought.

Having looked briefly at the issues of the sources and the prominence of Paul's teaching, let us now turn to the question, what is the essence of Paul's teaching on the return? We shall look first to 1 Thessalonians, which is his early and definitive statement, and at other references in the middle and later periods of his life.

First Thessalonians is pre-eminently the New Testament's book of the Second Coming. The subject is mentioned in every chapter, and dealt with exhaustively in one. We shall view the book not only as Paul's teaching about the return, but as a reflection of what Christians believed in the middle of the First Century. In chapter 1, Paul reminds the Thessalonians of how they "turned to God from idols, to serve a living and true God, and to wait for his Son from heaven." His language here was evidently misunderstood, for he had to write a second letter to explain that he meant *work and wait*, not *sit and wait* (see 2 Thess. 3:6). In chapter 2 he commends his readers, saying that they were his "joy or crown of boasting before our Lord Jesus Christ at his coming." The casual nature of the reference shows the extent to which the return was an accepted idea among all Christians. It was referred to as a fact which any

Christian knew. Chapter 3 contains a kind of benediction in which the apostle prays that God may establish their hearts "unblamable in holiness before our God and Father, at the coming of our Lord Jesus with all his saints." Again, the general acceptance of the return is obvious. Chapter 5 emphasizes the suddenness and unexpectedness of the event; the Lord will come "like a thief in the night." Because of this, Christians should "not sleep, as others do," but "keep awake and be sober." Also in chapter 5 is Paul's prayer that their "spirit and soul and body be kept sound and blameless at the coming of our Lord Jesus Christ." William Barclay observes that this means Paul "expected them to be in the body when Christ came; he expected the coming of Christ to be within their lifetime and his."[6]

It is chapter 4, however, that merits special attention. In one paragraph, Paul gives the quintessence of New Testament teaching on the return.

> But we would not have you ignorant, brethren, concerning those who are fallen asleep, that you may not grieve as others do who have no hope. For since we believe that Jesus died and rose again, even so, through Jesus, God will bring with him those who have fallen asleep. For this we declare to you by the Lord, that we who are alive, who are left until the coming of the Lord, shall not precede those who have fallen asleep. For the Lord himself shall descend from heaven with a cry of command, with the archangel's call, and with the sound of the trumpet of God. And the dead in Christ will rise first; then we who are alive, who are left, shall be caught up together with them in the clouds to meet the Lord in the air; and so we shall always be with the Lord. Therefore comfort one another with these words.
>
> (1 Thess. 4:13-18)

Several phrases claim our interest.
We who are alive . . . shall not precede those who are asleep

. . . the dead in Christ shall rise first. Here Paul reassures the Thessalonians who were concerned that Christians who had died recently would be left behind at Christ's coming. (We shall not treat seriously the waggish comment that the dead will rise first because they have a few feet farther to go!)

The Lord himself will descend from heaven . . . with the archangel's call, and with the sound of the trumpet of God. Many New Testament scholars would say that Paul is expressing his truth in symbolic form. If they are right, his language would be comparable to the words of Revelation in its description of heaven: golden streets, and twelve-fruited trees. For a Christian this kind of statement is certainly true, but not in a crudely literal way. It is true in the sense that it uses human language, inadequate though it may be, to express what is too wonderful for language to describe. Far from regarding such a statement as false, we might say that it is so true that our ordinary language simply cannot describe it, and we have to resort to picture-language. As C. S. Lewis notes, religious language (such as saying Jesus is the Son of God) is necessarily poetic, since the reality of which it speaks is outside our experience. But it is not merely an expression of emotion; it conveys information.[7]

Those who are alive . . . shall be caught up with them in the clouds to meet the Lord in the air. Much the same comment may be made here as about the apocalyptic language of the previous section. Paul is not talking about a heavenly elevator, or more contemporarily, a rocket carrying the true church to regions beyond. A dash of "reverent agnosticism" may be in order at this point. But at the same time, let us not spiritualize his message into a kind of beautiful but meaningless vapor. Unless we change Paul's name to Aesop or Grimm we must assume that he means what he says: that Christ, at his coming, will take us bodily to himself. The mechanics we may safely leave to God; the essential meaning is not in doubt. If our theology is so laden with cultural assumptions that it

cannot bear the clear intent of Paul's statement, so much the worse for our theology!

Therefore, comfort one another with these words. An elderly minister I knew as a youth had heard evangelist D. L. Moody preach on the return. He reported that after expounding the doctrine, Moody would always emphasize the comfort it should bring to Christians. And we would do well to stress this in the later Twentieth Century. For the doctrine of Christ's coming again as taught by many today is primarily to satisfy curiosity—often a morbid curiosity—or to prove some doctrinal point or establish a system of eschatological interpretation. But as taught by Paul, it was to bring comfort to disturbed Thessalonian Christians. The subject of this book will mean little to us until we have sensed the hopelessness of a history, personal or corporate, that is going nowhere. Reinhold Niebuhr wisely observes that it is only when we come to the end of ourselves that we find God.[8] It is when in some sense we have experienced the "dark valley" of which Sankey's hymn speaks that we can feel the throbbing strength of its line, "There'll be no dark valley *when Jesus comes.*"

In 1 Thessalonians we find the heart of Paul's teaching on the return. But in other later letters we can see the form the doctrine took in specific situations. We shall cover the various periods in Paul's writing career, to show that belief in the return is characteristic of not just the early period but of his entire life.

A familiar reference to the return is found in Paul's controversial chapter on marriage, 1 Corinthians 7, in which he counsels, "To the unmarried and widows I say that it is well for them to remain single as I do." More than one reason can be given for this advice. In Paul's day it was probably easier to serve Christ as a single person than as married. Can we imagine Paul with a wife and six children undertaking his rugged missionary journeys? This seems to be the thrust of Paul's thought when he says, "I want you to be free from anxieties . . . The married man is anxious about worldly affairs,

how to please his wife, and his interests are divided" (1 Cor. 7:32-33).

But the primary reason for his counsel to the Corinthians was what he and all of early Christianity believed to be the nearness of the return. "I think that in view of the present distress," writes Paul, "it is well for a person to remain as he is . . . The appointed time has grown very short . . . The form of this world is passing away" (1 Cor. 7:26-31). In essence, Paul tells them it would be better not to enter a permanent relationship such as marriage, since the coming of Christ is so near. Surely, then, in the (earlier) middle period of Paul's literary activity he had not lost his fervent belief in the nearness of Christ's return. Paul is telling them, as Barclay paraphrases it, to "order life on the assumption that the Second Coming was going to happen at any moment."

A somewhat later epistle in the middle period of Paul's writing was Romans. Though the return does not dominate his thought here in the same way it does in 1 Thessalonians or 1 Corinthians, the doctrine is still an important part of his thinking. He is like a composer who introduces a theme in the first movement of his symphony and then continues to use it is later movements, though in subtler and less obvious forms. Such a use of this theme is the paragraph beginning in Romans 13:11. Writing about Christian conduct—and more specifically, the place of love in that conduct—Paul argues that the imminence of the return should be a motive for high-level Christian living.

> "Another reason for right living is this: you know how late it is; time is running out. Wake-up, for the coming of the Lord is nearer now than when we first believed. The night is far gone, the day of his return will soon be here"   (Rom. 13:11-12 TLB).

The latest period of Paul's literary career was the time of his Roman imprisonment, near the end of his life. Was the

return as prominent then as at an earlier time in his spiritual development? The answer must be both Yes and No. Yes, he still believed firmly in the return, as we can see in what is probably the last book of this period, Philippians: "He who began a good work in you will bring it to completion at the day of Jesus Christ: (Phil. 1:6); "It is my prayer that . . . you may be pure and blameless for the day of Christ" (Phil. 1:9-10); "the day of the Lord is at hand" (Phil. 4:5). But Paul did not seem to think Christ would necessarily return in his lifetime. In the Philippian letter he discusses the alternative possibilities for him as a prisoner. "It is my eager expectation and hope that . . . Christ will be honored in my body, whether by life or by death." He then discusses these possiblities, saying he would rather go to be with Christ (in death), but he is still needed there. It is interesting that he does not consider the return of Christ as a third possibility. How different this is from 1 Thessalonians, in which he prays that his readers' *bodies* be kept sound at the coming of Christ (1 Thess. 5:23), that is, he assumes they will be alive when Christ returns.

A group of later writings of Paul are the Pastoral Epistles (Titus, 1 Timothy and 2 Timothy), about whose authorship and background there is much disagreement among scholars. However, biblical experts are inclining more to the Pauline authorship: witness the statement of Oxford's J.N.D. Kelly that the argument for the authenticity of the letters "tips the scales perceptibly . . . in favor of the traditional theory of authorship," and, "the present-day Christian is justified in assuming that they enshrine his [Paul's] authentic message."[9] The letter to Titus has an oft-quoted verse: We are to live soberly and godly "awaiting our blessed hope, the appearing of our great God and Savior, Jesus Christ" (2:13). But in 2 Timothy, and particularly chapter 4, we see a further example of what we saw in Philippians. Paul realizes that his death is near: "I am already on the point of being sacrificed; the time of my

departure has come" (2 Tim. 4:6). But there is still belief in
the return, for he charges Timothy "in the presence of God
and of Christ Jesus, who is to judge the living and the dead,
and by his appearing and his kingdom." The phrase "his
appearing" is a clear reference to the return, and "his
kingdom" to the regal rule of Christ. A similar reference is
2 Timothy 4:8 in which Paul states that a crown will be given
to him and also "to all who have loved his appearing." On
the other hand, if those scholars are right (which I doubt) who
say this is written by a disciple of Paul, it would still be very
significant, for it would show that not only Paul but his
followers retained a basic belief in the return of Christ.

In summary, Paul can be seen as both a reflector of primitive
Christian belief about the return, and one who refines, restates
and reshapes the doctrine. Though Paul in his last years seems
no longer to believe in the *immediacy* of Christ's coming, he
never wavers in his belief in its *factuality*. There is no reason
to doubt that Paul would feel comfortable saying
Maranatha—"our Lord, come"—at every period in his life
as a Christian.

THE SYNOPTIC GOSPELS AND CHRIST'S RETURN

The first three gospels, often called "synoptic" because they
"see together" the life of Christ, and the writings of Paul constitute the principal sources of the New Testament teaching
on the Second Coming. Having already looked at Paul, we
should be especially interested in how these books handle the
topic. One fact should be evident at the beginning: the gospels
are later than Paul. If there is any validity to the idea that the
later books have a somewhat different attitude toward the
return, we should expect to see that here. Also, though we
group the three books together because of basic similarity, we
need to remember that there are three different authors, writing
in varying situations and with different purposes. So we should
expect the basic Christian belief in the return to be used in a
way consonant with each author's special intention.

The synoptic Gospels' teaching on the return is found in both direct and indirect forms. The direct teaching is found mostly in the address given on the Mount of Olives, sometimes called the Olivet Discourse, or Apocalyptic Discourse, and also in occasional short sayings. The indirect teaching is found primarily in the parables, in which even a short phrase may reveal a particular author's viewpoint. We shall begin with the more obvious teaching, as found in the discourse, and supplement that with the less obvious, in the parables.

Mark — A Message of Expectancy

The background of the passages (Mark 13, Matthew 24, Luke 21) is well known. In the last days of his ministry, as Jesus and his disciples were leaving the temple, one of them expressed wonder at the stones of which it was built (not a surprising feeling; even modern visitors are amazed at Herod's buildings). Jesus responded by saying that one day all these stones would be thrown down. The disciples evidently pondered the meaning of this as they walked east, down into the valley and up the Olivet slope. Upon reaching the summit, Peter, James and John took him aside and asked when all this would happen, and what sign would precede it. In answer Jesus gave what is universally regarded as his supreme and definitive statement about his return.

However, before we look at it in some detail certain "ground rules" of interpretation must be laid down, since the material is so difficult. Perhaps the first thing to be said is that at least two separate topics are discussed here, and they are so much alike that they are easily confused. The immediate topic is the fall of Jerusalem, which would take place in 70 A.D., some forty years after Jesus spoke the words. Quite literally the stones would be "thrown down" by the Romans as they destroyed the city. The other topic is his Second Coming, of which the fall of Jerusalem would be a miniature or symbol. One reason these chapters cause so much confusion is that the two topics

are often not recognized as separate. Another assumption I shall make is that we really do hear the authentic voice of Jesus speaking in these chapters. This is not to ignore the background of the chapters in Jewish apocalypticism, nor the editorial coloring of the gospel authors; these will be taken into account. But I must believe that after stripping away the externals we shall come upon the thoughts of Jesus himself, in the same way that one unwraps a large Christmas box for the sake of the sometimes small but precious gift inside.

Our procedure will be to start with Mark's account (chapter 13), almost universally agreed to be the earliest, and then see what additions or changes Matthew and Luke made. We shall follow the paragraphing of the Revised Standard Version.

> The disciples ask, When will this (the destruction of the temple) be, and what signs shall we look for? Jesus tells them not to be led astray by false prophets. For there will be various catastrophic events—war, earthquake, famine—but this is not the end. (Mark 13:3-8)

> Jesus' followers will be persecuted, but God will help them and tell them what to say in moments of crisis.
> (Mark 13:9-13)

> When the "desolating sacrilege" appears, flee to the mountains, for there will be a time of unparalleled human suffering. (Mark 13:14-23)

> There will be signs in the heavens—sun and moon darkened, stars falling—after which the Son of Man will come in power. (Mark 13:24-27)

> When you see these things happening, know that "he is near, at the very gates." (Mark 13:28-31)

> None but the Father—not even the Son, or the angels—knows the day and hour of the Return. So we must be ready, and watch. (Mark 13:32-37)

It was already pointed out that one pitfall in the study of

the Olivet Discourse is the confusion of the fall of Jerusalem (70 A.D.) with the Second Coming. The former seems to be the theme of verses 14-20. The "desolating sacrilege" probably builds upon historical memories of the time Antiochus offered swine flesh upon the Jewish altar (168 B.C.). As Barclay sums it up, Jesus said, "Some day, quite soon, you will see the very incarnate power of evil, rise up in a deliberate attempt to destroy the people and the Holy place of God."[10] The evil power referred to is the Romans. But the return of Christ seems to be the subject of verses 7-8 and 24-27. In describing his coming Jesus used imagery already familiar from the Old Testament and the intertestamental writings: that the Day of the Lord (the Second Coming) will be preceded by wars, by signs in the heavens, and by the ingathering of the Jews. Not all would agree with Barclay that "the imagery we can disregard." But most would approve his conclusion, "the one thing we must retain is the fact that Jesus did foretell he would come again."

This, then is the picture in Mark. There is in this gospel a sense of imminence and immediacy; it could without exaggeration be called the gospel of *expectancy*. It should be of much interest to see how Matthew and Luke, writing later than Mark and with different purposes and perspectives, deal with the same basic material.

Matthew — A Message of Faithfulness

Matthew has little of special interest to add to Mark's account of the Olivet Discourse. The major supplement in Matthew (24) is the recognition of the common, business-as-usual character of life at the return, implying that the extraordinary will happen in the context of the ordinary. As in the time of Noah, people will be "eating and drinking, marrying and giving in marriage." Also, the unexpectedness of the return is made more dramatic, for at his coming "two men shall be in the field . . . two women will be grinding at the mill; one

is taken and one is left." The chapter ends with a short parable on watchfulness to be considered below.

The uniqueness of Matthew's view of the return is found more in certain parables than in the apocalyptic discourse. There are three, immediately following Matthew's account of the address, which bear on the subject. The first (Matt. 24:45-51) is the parable of the faithful and wise servant. It concerns a trusted servant who looks after his master's things while he is away. But if the master is *delayed*, another servant in the same position might act in an unworthy manner. In this case the master *will come back when he is not expected* and punish the rascal. The relation of this to the Second Coming is patent. The church is to be the faithful servant, not knowing when the Master will return, but always ready.

The parable of the wise and foolish maidens (Matt. 25:1-13) makes the same point in another way. In going to meet the bridegroom, five maidens brought oil for their lamps and five did not. But *the bridegroom was delayed*, and thus the foolish maidens ran out of oil. Finally, in desperation they tried to "crash" the wedding, but were told, "I do not know you." Jesus then appends the warning, "Watch therefore, for you know neither the day nor the hour."

The Parable of the Talents (Matt. 25:14-30) is well-known, and hardly needs to be retold here. It has to do with servants who were given different amounts of money, and either invested or hoarded it. The story is a beautiful lesson on how our lives can be used. But Matthew adds a seemingly irrelevant phrase, "Now *after a long time* the master of those servants came and settled accounts with them." The stress on the great length of time seems to have no particular function in the parable, except in an eschatological sense. It is usually regarded as the evangelist's way of reassuring the people of his day, impatient and perhaps discouraged that Christ has not yet returned, that the delay is part of God's plan. All three parables thus have a common theme: The master is *delayed*, and we must *be ready* when he comes.

Matthew also deals with the return in a more general way. If we take the parables immediately after Matthew 24 as related to the discourse, we can see the following sequence of thought: The church should not be sitting on its hands, watching for the great day, but should be watchful, using rather than burying its talents, and engaging in the performance of merciful acts (Matt. 25:31-46). One is reminded of Paul's advice to the Thessalonians: Wait for his coming, but work while you wait! This theme is reinforced in the Great Commission (Matthew 28:16-20), which commands the church to go and "make disciples of all nations." And if any Christian in the last quarter of the First Century thought of Christ as absent because he had not visibly returned, there is in the same passage the sublime promise, "Lo, I am with you always, to the close of the age." These are "the words of a gentleman, of the most strict and sacred honor," wrote David Livingstone in his diary. Christians of all times and places have agreed with him.

Luke and Acts — A Message of Caution

By a process of deduction, we might reason as follows about Luke's position on the return. Any later New Testament book (from about 80 A.D. on) will doubtless show concern for the problem of the delay of Christ's return. By general agreement, Luke-Acts was written somewhere between 80-85 A.D. So we would expect to find in Luke, as in Matthew, accommodation to and justification of the delay. Do we in fact find this in the third gospel?

The answer, I think, is a clear "Yes." A comparison of Mark's and Luke's accounts of the Olivet Discourse establishes the point well. The basic difference is on the question of *when* Christ will return.

> When you see these things taking place, you know that he is near, at the very gates. (Mark 13:28)

> Take heed that you are not led astray, for many will come in my name, saying . . . 'The time is at hand!' Do not go after them. (Luke 21:8)

> When you see these things taking place, you know that
> the kingdom of God is near.   (Luke 21:31)

Whereas in Mark the clear implication is that the return is near, Luke warns against those who say, "The time is at hand." And instead of saying "He is near," as in Mark, Luke has "the kingdom is near." While Luke's precise meaning may be open to question, one senses an obvious reluctance to say, "*He* is near." Is there a contradiction between Mark and Luke? No, simply different applications of the gospel for differing situations. Mark's answer may be more primitive and closer to what Jesus actually said, but Luke is also saying something needed in his time. This of course illustrates why we have four gospels instead of one; it was necessary that there be various applications and interpretations of the gospel for different times and places. The gospel writers, someone has said, sing in harmony, not in unison.

Other differences, though of less importance are also interesting. Probably speaking of the fall of Jerusalem, Mark records, "When you see the desolating sacrilege set up where it ought not to be, then let those in Judea flee to the mountains" (Mark 13:14). Luke has, "When you see Jerusalem surrounded by armies, then you shall know that its desolation is near." It is sometimes suggested that Luke can be as specific as this because at this point he writes history, not prophecy; that is, he has given an empirical description of the fall of Jerusalem, after the fact. Also, Luke omits the saying found in both Mark and Matthew, "Of that day and hour no one knows, not even the angels, nor the Son. . . ." Did the denial of this knowledge to Christ offend Luke's high christology? Another omission from Luke is the worldwide preaching of the gospel as a sign of Christ's coming, again found in both Mark and Matthew. Some commentators express surprise at this omission, since the author of the third gospel describes in Acts the systematic and increasing proclamation of the gospel

in the world. But it seems to me that Luke may be guarding against the danger of people saying that as soon as some specific area (such as Asia-Minor, Macedonia or Achaia) was evangelized, Christ would come. Evidently the author takes pains to leave no possible reasons for Christians to say, "The time is at hand."

Luke also makes an interesting point (Luke 12:35-40) in what seems to be a parallel to Matthew's parable of the wise and foolish maidens (Matt. 25:1-13). Be watchful and expectant, he writes, "like men waiting for their master to come home from the marriage feast." If the master comes "in the second watch, or in the third" and finds them awake and waiting, "blessed are those servants!" It is probably assumed in this passage that there were four watches in the night, the danger of sleep being greatest in the second and third. Thus Luke is more specific than Matthew, who had said only, "If the bridegroom is delayed. . . ." By mentioning the second and third watches Luke implies that the delay in Christ's return may be considerable.

Apart from the specifically eschatological passages, the gospel of Luke as a whole, and its companion volume, the Acts of the Apostles, seem to be built around Luke's reaction to the delay in Christ's return. By the time Luke wrote, in the eighth decade of the first century, it was perfectly obvious that from a human point of view there was a delay. Did this mean that something had gone wrong? Was subsequent history to be simply an anxious and empty waiting for Christ's coming? Certainly not, Luke implies. For God has given us the church; and its activity, under the guidance of the Holy Spirit, gives meaning and purpose to history until Christ comes again. Sometimes the ecclesiastical and eschatological strands in the New Testament are regarded as incompatible. Not so for Luke; Christ will come again, but until he does, he is working through his church.

The Book of Acts, the companion volume to the gospel of

Luke (both being written by the same person), does not particularly stress the return. This is not surprising, since, as we
have seen, one of Luke's major emphases is the delay of
Christ's coming. But neither can we say the subject is absent
from Acts. Peter's sermon at Pentecost quotes from the
prophet Joel concerning the signs in the heavens "before the
day of the Lord comes, the great and manifest day" (Acts
2:20). And the word of the "two men . . . in white robes"
after the Ascension will always be one of the strongest
statements of the return: "This Jesus, who was taken up from
you into heaven, will come in the same way as you saw him
go into heaven" (1:11). *This same Jesus*, not some figure of
wild imagination, not a semi-mythological personage from
Jewish or Christian mythology, but the one elsewhere called
"the man Christ Jesus." This should save us from making too
radical a distinction between the First and Second Comings
of Christ, for the One who *will come* is the same One who
has come. Any attempt to portray the Christ of the Second
Coming as fundamentally different from the Christ of Nazareth
and Calvary (a frequent tendency today among some who stress
the return) should be labeled sub-Christian, something more
of the old covenant than of the new.

THE GENERAL LETTERS

The general letters of the New Testament, by common
understanding written in the last two decades of the First
Century, reflect the lowered level of expectation that would
seem natural in that period. The various books all at some point
or points affirm their belief in the return—indeed, the nature
of the references to it indicate its universal acceptance among
all Christians—but in none of the books is it the main theme,
or even a main theme (though it comes closest to being so in
1 John). In these letters, we find solid acceptance of the doctrine, but no special emphasis.

Hebrews — Eagerly Waiting

Though not especially stressing the return, the letter to the Hebrews has one noteworthy reference to the subject. "So Christ having been offered once to bear the sins of many, will appear a second time, not to deal with sin but to save those who are eagely waiting from him" (Heb. 9:28). The author is thinking in terms of the Old Testament priesthood. The high priest goes into the sanctuary to effect atonement for the people. What if something should happen to him, so that he could not perform this all-important function? The people are relieved, then, when they see him emerge; they know that salvation has been procured. Similarly, Christ has gone into the heavenly sanctuary; and when he returns he will confirm our salvation, and will prove by his reappearance that he has put away sin. Also interesting is the fact that the author conceives of the purpose of the return as positive, "to save those who are eagerly waiting for Him"; the judgmental aspect, while true, is subordinated to the soteriological (Those who see the return only in terms of apocalyptic disaster, please note!). We may observe also that the Greek word commonly used for the return in Paul and the Gospels, *parousia*, is not used here, but the word *opthe*, "appearance," the same word Paul used to describe the various appearances of Christ after the Resurrection (1 Cor. 15:5). Thus Hebrews views the return as completing the series of revelations.

James — Patience In Waiting

Like other general letters that do not particularly stress the return, James shows his acceptance of the doctrine by several times referring to it. In this book the concept is mainly related to "patience."

> Be patient, therefore, brethren, until the coming of the Lord. Behold, the farmer waits for the precious fruit of the earth, being patient over it until it receives the early and the late rain. You also be patient. Establish your

> hearts, for the coming of the Lord is at hand. Do not
> grumble, brethren, against one another, that you may not
> be judged; behold, the Judge is standing at the doors.
>   (James 5:7-9)

The fact that James needs to stress patience shows that waiting for the return came to be increasingly a problem for Christians in the latter half—and especially the last quarter—of the first century. (This may have implications concerning the date of the letter of James; would an early letter need to counsel patience?) It is also helpful to see the context of the passage. In James 5:1-6 the author had been showing the vanity of riches and of earthly rewards. But as with the farmer waiting for harvest—"the precious fruits of the earth," worthy rewards will be given to those who wait patiently for his coming. And finally, James contributes a notable phrase to the whole discussion of the return: "Behold, the Judge is standing at the doors."

The phrase "the coming of the Lord is at hand" also raises an important point. In modern terms we would say that James is here affirming the *imminence* of the return. Imminence does not necessarily mean that something *will* happen soon, but only that it *may*. A newspaper headline saying WAR IS IMMINENT does not mean that inevitable war will break out soon. But it does mean that it *may* happen at any time. To say that Christ's return is imminent, then, is not to express a certainty, but to state a very real possibility (the *fact* of the return is of course certain for the Christian, but not the timing). In logical terms, it is conditional rather than categorical: it may happen very soon, but this is not to say that it will.

1 Peter—Preparation For Christ's Return

The letter known as 1 Peter is on the surface little concerned about the return. The book's main theme is the hope Christians have in the face of persecution. Paul, writing in 50 or

51 A.D., might have answered that our hope is Christ's coming. But in the middle sixties (or later, depending on one's view of the book's authorship and locale) 1 Peter centers the Christian hope in Christ's resurrection: "By his great mercy we have been born again to a living hope through the resurrection of Jesus Christ from the dead" (1 Peter 1:3). As in other books that do not seem to stress the return, there is nevertheless clear evidence of continued belief in the doctrine. "Gird up your minds, be sober," says the author; "Set your hope fully upon the grace that is coming to you at the revelation [return] of Jesus Christ" (1 Pet. 1:13). It is interesting that though he does not initially identify the Christian hope with the return, he cannot in this verse complete his discussion without alluding to it. Another clear reference is 1 Peter 4:7—"The end of all things is at hand; therefore keep sane and sober for your prayers" ("The end of the world is coming soon; therefore be earnest, thoughtful men of prayer"—TLB). The idea seems to be that the return is near, so be ready, through prayer and right living. J. H. Jowett suggests that in this verse are two of the features which characterize a life possessed by a healthy expectancy of the Lord's coming: "sound-mindedness and sobriety"; the former to keep us from "the destructiveness of panic," the latter to free us from a "feverish sensationalism."[11] Good advice, then and now!

The Letters of John—Comfort While Waiting

The letters of John were written toward the end of the first century, at a time when heresy and church organization were major problems in the Christian community. As in the other "general letters," the return is not in the forefront of their thinking. But it is still a cornerstone of Christian belief, even though cornerstones are not always easily seen or remembered.

A key idea in the first letter is manifestation. "History is manifestation," says Robert Law in his classic commentary, "each of its successive events being merely the emergence into

visibility of what already exists." So for John the Incarnation is not a new event in history but a manifestation of "what was from the beginning" (1 John 1:1); and the cross did not reveal God's love as a new reality but as a manifestation of the love that is at the heart of God's nature ("God is love"). The return, then, is a further aspect of this manifestation.

Another idea of 1 John, also prominent in Paul, is that the world is passing away. "The world passes away, and the lust of it" (1 John 2:17). Christians are living in "the last hour," which can be understood as either the gospel age as a whole, or a special crisis period near its end. False teachers, or antichrists, have arisen: "Many antichrists have come; therefore we know it is the last hour" (1 John 2:18). The return (again quoting Law) will not be the arrival of one who is absent, but "the self-revealing of one who is present"; it will be "a different mode of self-revelation on the part of Christ." It will not be so much an intrusion from beyond as a dramatically clearer focus upon him who has been at work among us all along.

In what must surely be one of the richest meditations in all the New Testament, John explores in depth the meaning of the return.

> Beloved, we are God's children now; it does not yet appear what we shall be, but we know that when he appears we shall be like him, for we shall see him as he is. And every one who thus hopes in him purifies himself, as he is pure.
>
> (1 John 3:2)

"What we shall be" is what we are now, God's children. All that we will be is present in us now, in embryo, so to speak. At his coming we shall see him—not the *deus absconditus* of Job or of classical mysticism, not the "God-in-Himself" of Erigena or the "superessential indetermination" of pseudo-Dionysius—but Jesus, "as he is." And seeing him, "we shall be like him." At the return, suggests Law, there will be

"sudden development"; as seeds lying dormant for many years in a barren plain suddenly begin to grow after a desert shower, the latent traits in the believer will develop at His coming; the "buds of earth" will become "flowers of heaven."[12] While admittedly we do not and perhaps cannot at this time know the full meaning of those words, they reveal another aspect of the return that comforts the spirit and stimulates the mind!

First John also raises an issue not always considered in thinking about the return—its ethical implications. After the biblical passage considered above the author says, "Every one who thus hopes in him is purified, even as he is pure." The truths implicit in such a statement are manifold, and I would not presume to say that I have discovered them all. But I am reminded of a wall plaque, seen in my youth, which had some such message as this: "I don't want to be doing, thinking or saying anything that I would be ashamed of when Jesus comes." A bit negative, perhaps, but the essential idea is good. If Christ may come at any time—indeed, if His return will take place when we do not expect it, and will take us completely by surprise—then at all times we shall want to be doing what he would approve at his coming.

Any discussion of the letters of John must surely at some point involve the other great Johannine writing, the gospel of John. It may surprise some to see only a few paragraphs given to what may be the greatest book in the Bible. There are at least two reasons for this. One is that we could not do justice to it in the few pages that would be allotted to it in this short book. And the other is that this gospel is probably less concerned with the return than almost any other book in the New Testament. It deals with the subject in its own unique and fascinating way; but would certainly not be regarded by even the most ardent Second Coming enthusiast as a major book on the issue.

The gospel of John is perhaps best understood when given the title applied to it by one of the early church fathers, Clement

of Alexandria, who called it "the spiritual gospel." Basic to this gospel is the fact that it "spiritualizes" events. It not only relates the real, space-time historical event, but also gives the spiritual or symbolic meaning. For example, other gospels tell of Jesus feeding the five thousand. John also recounts the story, but follows it with the discourse in which Jesus says, "I am the bread of life" (John 6), thus subtly making a connection between bread for the body (feeding the multitude) and bread for the soul (Christ as the bread of life).

In the same way, John spiritualizes the return of Christ. In his Upper Room Discourses (John 14-16) Jesus promises: "I will not leave you desolate; I will come to you . . . But the Counselor, the Holy Spirit, whom the Father will send in my name, he will teach you all things, and bring to your remembrance all that I have said to you . . . He [the Counselor] will glorify me, for he will take what is mine and declare it to you" (John 14:18, 25; 16:14). Many scholars take these words to mean that John sees Christ as in a sense having returned in the Holy Spirit. This would in no way deny the fact of an objective, end-of-time Second Coming. But it would be John's way of saying, to a generation that looked for that coming and had been disappointed: "Look; Christ has not yet come in his final, glorious return. But do not think he is absent, for in a sense he has already come, in the Holy Spirit."

To sum up the contributions of the gospel and letters of John, we may say that the Johannine writings interpret the event from the standpoint of immanence rather than transcendence. Whereas in Paul and the synoptic Gospels there is the thought of an ascended Christ who will come back, the Johannine Christ is one who is already here, in the Holy Spirit, and will further manifest himself in the event we know as the Second Coming. However, a word of caution should be given. This contrast should not be taken as absolute, for there are elements of immanence in Paul and the Synoptics, and of transcendence in John.

Fortunately we do not have to choose between the two emphases; from the standpoint of the New Testament as a whole they are both true. For although in ordinary life "different" often means "conflicting" (as in the contrast between capitalism and communism), in the Bible "different" usually means "complementary" as in the four different views of Jesus in the four gospels. So we see here "different" views of his coming, but only in the sense that each adds detail without which the total picture would be incomplete.

2 Peter — The Assurance of Christ's Return

Two things can be said about the Book of 2 Peter. It is regarded by some as one of the latest books of the New Testament. However, a case can be made for Petrine authorship (and hence an earlier dating), as when R. H. Mounce observes[13] that the supposed doctrinal differences between 1 and 2 Peter turn out rather to be "variations in emphasis resulting from the immediate needs of the congregations," and that those who emphasize the stylistic differences draw conslusions that go beyond the data. The other thing to be said is that it is one of the least read and least esteemed books of the Bible. This is unfortunate. I would agree that it does not compare with a Romans or gospel of John, or even a Philippians or 1 Peter. But that does not render it of no value. Whether it is one of the "very late" books of the New Testament, written at a time when the "first fine careless rapture" of early Christianity had cooled down and become less rapturous, or rather simply a "later" New Testament book coming out of the mid-sixties in the first century, it is to be classified among the later New Testament writings. Whether we adopt a "consensus" or conservative view of the date, then, it is to be regarded as a later book. What did the Christians of *that* time believe, and more specifically, what was *their* view of the return? Had they become disillusioned and discouraged because the expected event had not happened?

Judging from 2 Peter chapter 3, we would say that they had.
"You must understand," says the author, "that scoffers will
come in the last days . . . saying, 'Where is the promise of
his coming'?" The writer's answer to the scoffer's question
is what J. H. Jowett calls "the leisureness of God." God is
not on our time schedule, thus "with the Lord one day is as
a thousand years and a thousand years as one day" (3:8). If
we seek a motive for the delay, it is that God "is forbearing
toward you, not wishing that any should perish, but that all
should reach repentance." God's leisureness, Jowett continues,
is "not of heedlessness, but of mercy."[14] If God settled all
his accounts promptly, none of us would have a chance!

A further emphasis is one seen already in other General
Letters—the ethical implications of the return. "Seeing that
all these things [the heavens and the earth] are thus to be
dissolved, what sorts of persons ought you to be in lives of
holiness and godliness, waiting for and hastening the coming
of the day of God." In a way, 2 Peter speaks particularly to
our age at this point. We are not so interested in the *how* of
his coming; indeed, many of us feel that no literal description
of his coming could ever be given. But we are very interested
in what might be called the existential meaning of the return:
What does it mean to my daily life? No "pie-in-the-sky"
answer, this; that Christ may come at any time means that I
must be honest, hard working and sincere in all my dealings,
"an example," as another New Testament writer puts it, "in
speech and conduct, in love, in faith, in purity" (1 Tim. 4:12).
Thus the "late" view of 2 Peter is in essence the same as the
"early" view of Paul; Christians are to "wait for his son from
heaven" (1 Thess. 1:10), but are also to "shun any brother
living in idleness" and "to do their own work in quietness and
to earn their own living" (2 Thess. 3). So there *is* a connection between ethics and apocalypse, between what we should
do for God and what he will one day do for us!

REVELATION – HOPE IN SUFFERING

I hope that in my discussion of Revelation I do not lose those readers who have stayed with me to this point. For doubtless some were looking forward to this last book of the Bible as a climax to the entire study. I would agree that it makes a fitting climax to the New Testament as a whole. Whether or not it is such a peak for our subject, however, depends on one's view of the book's essence. For some, such as Hal Lindsey, Revelation is really history written ahead of time, with the return as the culmination of it all. To those of this persuasion the mysterious symbols of the book are all pointing very specifically to events leading up to his appearance.

This is at present a widely held and honored point of view, one from which I would dissent only for the most compelling reasons. But for me there are such reasons, and thus I must dissent in favor of the other major view, represented by the majority of contemporary biblical scholars. This is that the book was written, not to describe the events to happen in all the future, but to interpret the meaning of what was happening during the time of the author. What was happening was a violent persecution; and on the contemporary view the symbols (such as the two beasts of chapter 13 rising from the sea, and the beast numbered 666) describe the events at the time, rather than those of a distant future.

With this understanding of the book, then, I see it as certainly sharing the commonly held Christian belief in the return, but making no massive or unique contribution on the subject. The book begins by stating its purpose as showing "what must soon take place." Christians are to read and obey it because "the time is near." The events referred to in these phrases are understood by many to be Christ's return, though some (e.g. Caird) disagree. It is probable that in the Letters to the Seven Churches (Rev. 2-3) the "coming" of Christ sometimes refers to other than his final return (Rev. 2:16; 3:3); but some references may well be to his ultimate coming (Rev. 2:25; 3:11).

One of these, Revelation 3:11, seems especially noteworthy: "I am coming soon; hold fast what you have, so that no one may seize your crown." It seems the kind of message a military rescue unit might radio to some beleaguered fellow-soldiers, "Hold on; don't lose all you have gained; we are coming soon." It is not always easy to separate the *near* from the *ultimate* coming of Christ in the Book of Revelation.

About chapter 19, though, there seems little doubt. It is the dramatic climax of the book; and if the return is referred to at all in any major section of the book, surely it is here. However, the doctrine is stated symbolically rather than literally. The non-specialist might have trouble recognizing it as the return described by Paul, the Synoptics or almost any other part of the New Testament. But this by no means negates its power as an ultimate statement of encouragement to suffering Christians. The Book of Revelation could be described as a book of comings of Christ, culminating in the Coming of Christ. As J. P. M. Sweet so well puts it, "The heavenly worship . . . dissolves into the reality it celebrates"[15]; that is to say, the celebration of the return "dissolves" into the return itself. The imagery of the chapter is powerful. Christ rides a white horse, judges and makes war, has eyes like a flame of fire, is clad in a robe dipped in blood, and leads the white-clad armies of righteousness. Heaven is now opened (v. 11) and "God breaks out into the world" (Sweet). This "open heaven" seems the author's way of representing what Paul describes as Christ's descent from heaven at the archangel's call (1 Thess. 4:16).

The clearest references I see to the return are in the last chapter (22) of the book. In Revelation 22:10 Christ says (through an angel), "Do not seal up the words of the prophecy of this book, for the time is near." This is similar to passages in Paul and elsewhere stating that the return is close at hand. In Revelation 22:12 Christ speaks again: "Behold, I am coming soon, bringing my recompense, to repay every one for what

he has done." Here is the judgmental aspect of the return, which we have seen in other writers. However, the positive as well as the negative side of judgment may be implied here, the distribution of rewards as well as of punishments. And finally, there is the glorious ending of the book—and of the Bible—in Revelation 22:20: "He who testifies to these thing says, 'Surely I am coming soon.' Amen. Come, Lord Jesus!" We cannot imagine a better way to end a book designed to lift the spirits of suffering Christians; and perhaps we twentieth century Christians, beset with problems and sufferings of our own, should consider making their hope our hope!

IN SUMMARY

We have seen that the New Testament is replete with references to Christ's Second Coming, and that its writers saw that belief as resting on Old Testament foundations. In the great symphony that we call the New Testament there are two themes, as in a movement of a Haydn or Mozart symphony. The first is that Christ *has* come; the second is that he will come *again*. Variations of these appear (the role of the church, Christian ethics, the Christian and the state, etc.) but always in relation to the two great themes. Christians have been willing, even eager, to play and replay the first theme; but the second theme has been little heard, except in the cacaphanous setting of cultism or extremism. The purpose of this book is to help restore this theme to its rightful place in God's music, in which it is neither ignored nor distorted through overemphasis.

Three stages can be observed in the attitude of New Testament writers toward the return. The earliest books, including Paul's first letters and perhaps the gospel of Mark, see the return as something to be expected at any moment. The books of the middle period do not have the primitive expectancy of the earliest, but reflect a feeling that the coming, though a certainty, has been delayed. These would include Matthew and

Luke, Paul's later writings, and most of the General Letters. The late books, written near the end of the first century, try to help people understand the delay by various reasonings (I suppose the non-Christian would call them rationalizations). I am thinking mainly of 2 Peter's argument that God is not on our time scale and has delayed to give us time to repent; and of John's implication that in a sense Christ has come in the Holy Spirit.

If a value judgment be allowed, I want to say most emphatically that we Christians should not be ashamed of the doctrine of the return. We need not be ashamed, for example, that the early Christians were mistaken about the *timing* of the return. The *when* is a completely different question from the *what*. The *what* (His coming) was revealed. One could hardly reject it and still be a Christian in the historic sense. The *when* (the time of his coming) was not revealed, and was simply a matter of opinion among the early Christians. It happens that the earliest Christians with virtual unanimity believed the coming would be in their own lifetime; it also happens that they were wrong. So medieval Christians were wrong in believing in a geocentric astronomy; so Christians have since often been wrong in opposing what was later shown to be true in medicine, psychology, geology and many other areas. We do not lose our faith over these errors, nor should we over the early church's mistaken idea of when Christ would come.

Neither should we be ashamed of the doctrine because of its misuse and abuse by cultists. *Abusus non tollit usum*, says a Latin proverb; "Abuse does not destroy legitimate use." We should no more be ashamed of or ignore the belief because of cultist abuse than we should give up vitamins because food faddists have overstressed them, or keep our cars in the garage because a few lunatics drive cars badly. In practice most Christians have reacted to the extreme of overemphasis by going to the extreme of *no* emphasis. My point in this book is that we should avoid both, and recapture the power and beauty

of the primitive Christian message, "He is coming again."
Maranatha! "Come, Lord Jesus!"

Part Two

The Time of His Return

"We cannot possibly find out when [he will return]."

—C. S. Lewis, *The World's Last Night*

The first section established that the doctrine of the return is an indispensable element in Christian belief, and is a part of the "package" of affirmations we accept when we put our faith in Christ. This is confirmed, incidentally, by a study of the classical Christian creeds and confessions of faith. Each of them—Roman, Orthodox or Protestant— affirms in its way this basic article of Christian belief. Typical is the well-known statement of the (so-called) Apostles Creed: "He ascended into heaven, whence he shall come to judge the quick and the dead." A "Christianity" without this article of faith would surely be an emasculated, mutilated affair, unworthy of the name Christian.

C. S. Lewis's second thesis regarding the return is that (1) though as Christians we have absolute confidence that He will come, (2) we cannot possibly find out when. This will be explored in several ways, using Scripture, church history, biblical criticism, theology and contemporary religious life. We shall be distinguishing between the *fact* of His coming, which for the Christian is certain, and the *timing* of his coming, which (as Jesus said) is most uncertain.

CHAPTER 3

Comfort and Caution

Of that day and hour no one knows, not even the angels in heaven, nor the Son, but only the Father.
(Mark 13:32; Matt. 24:36)

It is one of the most surprising of all the statements of Jesus in the Olivet discourse. Luke omits this statement, perhaps because it offended his high Christology. It is also instructive to see what Christians since New Testament times have done with the words. Early Christian manuscript-copyists evidently had trouble with it, as some of them omitted "nor the son"; however, it is in the best manuscripts, and is considered authentic. Biblical scholars have struggled to accommodate this verse into the general system of Christian belief. One observes that it was a rebuke to idle curiosity, a way of saying to mankind, "It's none of your business." Another observes that the lack of knowledge was "economic" only, that is, it was in God's economy or plan that while on earth Christ would not do all that would be in his power as the Son, Second Person of the

Godhead. A nineteenth century critic, Schmiedel, saw this as one of only five sayings in all the Gospels that could be considered authentic, since no Christian would manufacture words that would seem to lessen Jesus' importance. But A. B. Bruce has the most helpful comment, seeing in the passage both comfort (my coming will be soon) and caution (but not as soon as you or I may think).[16] Comfort and caution—not a bad summary of all Jesus' words about his coming!

What was Paul's attitude toward this saying? He does not comment directly on it, but surely he must have approved it. For when he writes, in perhaps the greatest christological passage in the entire New Testament, that Jesus in his incarnation "emptied himself, taking the form of a servant" (Phil. 2:7), he was surely laying the foundation for a realistic and (in the best sense of the term) humanistic view of the infleshness of God in Christ. If that passage in Paul means anything at all, it is that Christ in his incarnation truly did become human, and in doing so must have surrendered for a time the exercise of certain divine powers. In the light of Philippians 2, then, this strange-sounding—and to some almost destructive—saying of Jesus makes perfectly good sense. By his own admission he did not know when he would return.

WHAT ABOUT DATE SETTING?

The saying we have been considering should be a caution and warning to us not to engage in date setting. This is reinforced by a theme that is found in Paul, the synoptic Gospels and the General Epistles: the idea of *unexpectedness*, often expressed by some form of the phrase, "thief in the night." For example, Paul tells the Thessalonians, "You yourselves know well that the day of the Lord will come like a thief in the night" (1 Thess. 5:2); and again, "You are not in darkness, brethren, for that day to surprise you like a thief" (1 Thess. 5:4). Matthew, shortly after recording the saying that only the Father knows the day, observes that we should be watchful,

"for you do not know on what day your Lord is coming." He then adds, "But know this, that if the householder had known in what part of the night the thief was coming, he would have watched and would not have let his house be broken into." He concludes: "Therefore you must also be ready; for the Son of man is coming at an hour you do not expect" (Matt. 24:41-44). Similar references are found in Luke (Luke 12:39) and Mark (Mark 13:33-37).

So we see that the early and "middle" books of the New Testament have the theme of the unexpectedness of the return. But what of the later books? Probably none is later than 2 Peter, which also has its version of the theme: "The day of the Lord will come like a thief, and then the heavens will pass away with a loud noise . . ." (2 Peter 3:10). It is interesting that the very earliest and the very latest books, Thessalonians and 2 Peter, both stress this idea. One can imagine contrary arguments that such an emphasis should characterize the early books because of their strong expression of the imminence of his coming or the later books because of the need to reassure people, disappointed at the delay, that the return was still very much on God's agenda, though the timing could never be known. The fact that such a theme runs through the New Testament—Paul and the Gospels; early and late books— certainly authenticates it as a major and primitive New Testament emphasis.

WHAT ABOUT SIGNS OF CHRIST'S COMING?

Closely related to the unexpectedness of Christ's return are the signs of his coming as given by Jesus. Various listings are recorded in the synoptic Gospels; I shall enumerate them with special concern for the books in which they are found. Common to all three gospels are the following: false Messiahs (Mark 13:6 and parallels), wars and rumors of wars (Mark 13:7-8), natural disasters (Mark 13:8), persecution (Mark 13:9), the "desolating sacrilege" (Mark 13:14; Luke's parallel in 21:10

in only partial, and may not be a parallel at all), and signs in the heavens (Mark 13:24). Common to Matthew and Mark, but omitted in Luke, is worldwide evangelization (Mark 13:10), a sign regarded by even quite liberal New Testament critics as having the ring of authenticity. Paul and in a lesser sense John (in the letters) add the appearance of antichrist or "the man of wickedness" (2 Thess. 2; 1 John 2:18-22).

Various questions arise in regard to these signs. Are they to come only at the end of the whole period? One immediate observation is that the expression "last times" or "last days" is commonly used in the New Testament to refer to the whole of the present epoch, not just the end of it. Many people have been taught that the last days refer to a period of apostasy and degeneracy near the end of the "church age." But the New Testament speaks otherwise. "In these last day," says the author of Hebrews, "God has spoken to us by his Son (Heb. 1:1). "Children, it is the last hour," writes John in his first letter (1 John 2:18). We must conclude that since there is no clear instance in which the New Testament writers single out the end of the present age as a time of special trouble and world chaos, the signs must be regarded as characteristic of the whole epoch in which we live, not just of its final segment.

A more serious question concerns the legitimacy of the emphasis on signs. Are "signs" compatible with the main emphases of Jesus' teachings? Some, usually those on the liberal side of New Testament criticism, argue in the negative, pointing to passages in which Jesus seems to condemn sign-seeking. Especially notable is the encounter with the Pharisees, who were seeking a sign from heaven "to test him." Jesus' reaction was that he "sighed deeply in his spirit and said, Why does this generation seek for a sign? Truly, I say to you, no sign shall be given to this generation" (Mark 8:11-12). On the face of it, this passage alone would seem to settle the issue: Jesus was opposed to signs.

But it can be pointed out that this was a situation of intense

hostility; to *them* ("Pharisees," in Mark; "Pharisees and Sad-
ducees," in Matthew) no sign would be given. Their mentality
was that of seeking God in the abnormal, a tendency Jesus
clearly opposed. Indeed, in his own temptation he had rejected
doing the abnormal or unusual to achieve his goals.

Jesus' reaction to their request is striking, in that it was not
only spiritual but physiological: "he sighed deeply in his spirit"
("gave a deep groan,"—TODAY'S ENGLISH VERSION; "with a sigh
that came straight from his heart."—JERUSALEM BIBLE). His
sigh seems to have been prompted by a combination of anger
and sorrow—anger at their general obtuseness, and sorrow at
their unbelief. If we take seriously the human nature of Jesus
it seems reasonable to assume that he had "had it" with those
people, had reached the limits of human endurance, and was
in effect saying, "with such an attitude, no sign will be given
to *you*!"

More positively, it should also be noted that the giving of
signs was a common Old Testament practice. Gideon twice
sought signs, and was given them (Judges 6:36-40). Hezekiah
was given a sign involving the reversal of the sundial's shadow
(2 Kings 20:8-11). And in a passage famous because of its messianic implications, Isaiah encourages King Ahaz, fearful
because of an invasion of Judah by nations to the north, to
"ask a sign of the Lord your God; let it be as deep as Sheol
or high as heaven" (Isa. 7:11). Ahaz refuses the sign; so the
prophet says, "The Lord himself will give you a sign"—the
birth of a child, Immanuel, with all the messianic overtones
of the name. It is doubtless true that the emphasis on signs
decreases as we move closer to the New Testament with its more
spiritual, more inward orientation. But there is no good reason
to say arbitrarily that Jesus had no place for them. Many of
us will remember from catechetical training that one of the
"offices" of Christ is that of prophet. And the prophet often
pointed to signs.

The most critical question concerning the signs, however,
is how they are related to the emphasis on the unexpectedness

of the return. The two would seem to be mutually exclusive: If there are signs, we know when to expect Him; if He is to return "like a thief in the night"—well, thieves do not usually send calling cards ahead. This is so serious an issue that some students of the problem feel we have to make a choice between the two, that there is no possible way they can be reconciled. Others, like the venerable Louis Berkhof (who terms the problem one of a return both imminent and distant), accept both but frankly admits that they seem incompatible and can be accepted together only on the basis of sheer faith.[17] Let us hope there are better solutions than either of these!

One suggestion, emanating mainly from the more liberal schools of New Testament criticism, is that since they seem incompatible we should retain the "thief in the night" emphasis and forget about the signs, which were evidently added to Jesus' teachings by well-meaning Christians. It is interesting that the dispute is only with the "signs"; all sides agree on the validity of the "unexpectedness" theme. The main arguments for the position are Jesus' seeming aversion to signs (as discussed above), and the fact that the writings between the Old and New Testaments abound in signs-literature. The implication is that the early Christians found this emphasis in those intertestamental books, rather than in the authentic teaching of Jesus. This is certainly a possible answer to the problem, but is purchased at too high a price—the integrity of the gospel record. To those who are committed to a Scripture that is more than just a casual, humanly-made collection of Jesus' sayings, a sort of spiritual "Poor Richard's Almanac," perhaps, there must be a better answer.

A more acceptable solution might be one that I somewhat surprisingly find myself sharing with Hal Lindsey, that the signs are meant to give only the most general indication of the time of His coming. It could be likened to a sign on the open range to watch for cattle. It alerts the driver to the possibility of animals on the road, though one could drive for many miles

before any are encountered. Or to change the illustration, it is like the medieval clocks that had an hour hand but no minute hand. A person would gain a very general idea of the time, but be unaware of the specific moment. This could be a possible solution as long as the "hour hand" were understood to represent a large historical epoch, and not a specific year or decade.

This leads to another solution, following closely from the preceding one, that a sign has meaning only in its relation to other signs, and especially in its *intensification*. An even casual look at the signs as given a few pages back should convince a person that they are not unique: war, natural disaster, persecution, to name a few. It would be hard to make a plausible case that there has been an *increase* in the occurrence of these events. Instead, the picture is mixed. Probably there are fewer wars now than of old, but they are bigger and more devastating when they come. Natural disasters still occur, but science and technology can to some extent predict and alleviate them. However, because of the larger number of people involved, they may sometimes be worse than in the past. Persecution still exists in the world, and sometimes with subtle refinements that would make even a Sennacherib or a Torquemada gasp; but surely it does not continue on the scale experienced in ancient times.

If the signs are not unique, then, they would not in themselves tell us of Christ's coming. But their intensification may do what individual signs do not. The whole, or aggregate, is different from the sum of its parts. An earthquake, a famine, a devastating plague—these by themselves would have little or no eschatological significance. But a combination of them could be a different story. Consider the following headlines in your morning newspaper—all on the same day:

**ENERGY CRISIS BRINGS WORLDWIDE
UNEMPLOYMENT, HUNGER
UNKNOWN PLAGUE KILLS MILLIONS ACROSS EUROPE
SOVIETS THREATEN WAR IN SOUTHERN AFRICA
TEL–AVIV CONSIDERS H-BOMB FOR DAMASCUS
ASTERIOD ON COLLISION COURSE WITH EARTH**

You might conclude that God was saying something! Certainly such a constellation of cataclysmic events could be regarded as a possible sign. But even here we must be careful, for such a combination of headlines is possible (though not probable) quite apart from any special theological meaning. At the very least, however, such a front page should make us remember Jesus' command, "Lift up your heads," for perhaps our "redemption is drawing near" (Luke 21:28).

A further interpretation of the signs was given in a sermon by Prof. T. F. Torrance, of Edinburgh. "They are not signs that tell when He will come, but signs and pledges telling us unmistakably that the end will come."[18] Professor Stephen Travis, in a recent book, has a similar opinion. "They are signs that the end is on its way, but not signs which enable us to work out God's timetable"; they were given by Jesus "to warn his followers about the troubles and challenges that lay ahead of them."[19] Thus understood, the signs would be strings of remembrance tied around the fingers of history, to remind us that history is moving toward divinely-appointed goals, to be culminated in the coming of the Prince himself. They remind us also of the insufficiency of history, that apart from this divine culmination, history is sterile, impotent, "dead in the water." History can be seen as "His story" only when "His Return" is its culminating chapter.

A final thought on this issue is to recognize its paradoxical nature. At its worst, paradox can be an evasion, as when a philosophy professor of mine, pressed into a corner on a difficult question, would retort, "But this is mystical!" But it also has an honorable and indeed biblical association. As Christians we live with the paradox of divine sovereignty and human freedom, of a Christ both human and divine, of a God both among us and beyond us. Paradox is not ultimate contradiction, but a way of holding two different truths that are both part of a larger truth. Or as someone has put it, paradox is truth standing on its head for emphasis. In relation to the

return, then, we Christians live with two sides of a great truth. Christ's return cannot be predicted or calculated in any way, but God gives us signs to remind us to be ready.

Perhaps by this time the reader is lost in a maze of explanations. Let me give my own synthesis of the different views, in hope of aiding the perplexed. I must agree with those who say that the "thief in the night" emphasis is the basic eschatological theme of the New Testament; *that* He will come, not *when*, is what is important. The "signs," however, are pledges and reminders that the end will come, but with no connotation of the timing. However, I cannot bring myself wholly to surrender *any* temporal meaning to the signs. I must believe that in the concatenation and intensification of the signs, though not in the appearance of any one by itself, there could be temporal implications. But such implications would be of only the most general nature; they would lead us not to set dates but to set our houses in order. The signs would remind us that "the Son of Man is coming at an hour you do not expect"; therefore, whatever may be the time of his coming, *we must be ready*.

CHAPTER 4

What About the Millennium?

One topic that almost always emerges when we talk about Christ's return is the Millennium. Since it is especially relevant to the *time* of his coming, we shall discuss it here.

There is one passage, Revelation 20:1-6, that is the origin of the concept of millennium, or thousand-year period. Other Scriptures are often associated with it, but they do not specifically mention the thousand years. Here, then, is the *locus classicus* of the doctrine.

> Then I saw an angel coming down from heaven, holding in his hand the key of the bottomless pit and great chain. And he seized the dragon, that ancient serpent, who is the Devil and Satan, and bound him for a thousand years, and threw him into the pit, and shut it and sealed it over him, that he should deceive the nations no more, till the thousand years were ended. After that he must be loosed for a little while.
>
> Then I saw thrones, and seated on them were those to whom judgment was committed. Also I saw the souls of

those who had been beheaded for their testimony to Jesus and for the word of God, and who had not worshipped the beast or its image and had not received its mark on their foreheads or their hands. They came to life, and reigned with Christ a thousand years. The rest of the dead did not come to life until the thousand years were ended. This is the first resurrection. Blessed and holy is he who shares in the first resurrection! Over such the second death has no power, but they shall be priests of God and of Christ, and they shall reign with him a thousand years. And when the thousand years are ended, Satan will be loosed from his prison and will come out to deceive the nations.

(Rev. 20:1-8)

WHAT IS PREMILLENNIALISM?

As most Christians know, eschatologists have formulated three interpretations of this passage. One is the premillennial (or, as the early church called it, chiliast) position, that Christ will come *before* the thousand years. Premillennialists are not agreed on the exact order of events immediately preceding the Millennium. Most believe there will be a seven-year period called the Great Tribulation, but they divide on *when* he will come in relation to the Tribulation. There are pre-tribulational, mid-tribulational and post-tribulational positions ("Post-tribulational premillennialism"—this should make the most zealous advocates of government gobbledegook green with envy!). Many premillennialists see the return as an event with two parts: Christ first comes *for* his saints (before, during or after the Tribulation) and then *with* his saints to rule for a thousand years. The world will have become so evil that only the King can save it from itself. He will rule in righteousness and peace for the millennial age, after which "Satan will be loosed from his prison" (Rev. 20:7) and will make an unsuccessful attempt to defeat God. Premillennialism has been a persistent minority point of view through the history of Christianity.

Sometimes it has been a vehicle for the expression of extremism, as in Montanism and some radical Anabaptist sects, but it is important to note that this is not *necessarily* so. Modern premillennalism divides into two basic groups: the dispensationalists (of which Hal Lindsey is a representative) and the moderate or classical school, represented in the last century by such scholars as Alford, Ellicott, Delitzsch and Godet, and in our century by such biblical interpreters as C. R. Erdman and probably Robert E. Speer. In other words, the Lindsey type of premillennialism that makes headlines today does not represent the movement as a whole.

WHAT IS POSTMILLENNIALISM?

The second group, the postmillennialists, see Christ coming *after* the Millennium. In comparison to the other views, postmillennialism is a relatively recent development. Though some find traces of one form of it in the medieval period, its most characteristic expression has been in the last few centuries. There are sharp divisions within this school—so sharp that it may be difficult to find real unity in the school of thought. One segment is very liberal religiously, and sees the "Millennium" as a time of cultural evolution, leading to a kingdom of God largely social in nature. The other group is very orthodox, and teaches the coming of the kingdom through the proclamation of the gospel in a doctrinally pure church. In spite of their diversity they agree—against premillennialism— that Christ will not be on earth during the Millennium (often interpreted as a symbol rather than as a literal thousand-year period). The earlier twentieth century liberal theologians of the University of Chicago would represent the liberal school; and J. G. Machen and B. B. Warfield, of early twentieth century Princeton Seminary, the orthodox.

WHAT IS AMILLENNIALISM?

The third position, amillennialism (literally, "no-millennialism"), finds no biblical or rational support for either

pre- or postmillennialism, but argues that the Millennium, being found in the highly symbolic book or Revelation, must itself be symbolic. God's plan for history does not involve a thousand-year break at any point. As the Apostles' Creed puts it, "He ascended into heaven, from whence he shall come to judge the quick and the dead." According to the creed there is no major event on God's historical agenda between Ascen sion and Final Judgment or the Second Coming. The creed says nothing about a millennium, finding support in the immense authority of St. Augustine. This became the major millennial tradition in the history of Christianity.

What does all this have to do with the question of the *time* of his coming? The answer depends on which millennial view one adopts. Premillennialists, especially of the dispensational variety, are prone to set dates or general time periods. I well remember a speaker in my youth who confidently said that he was sure the Lord would come in the lifetime of most of those present. Since then, he and most of that audience have passed to the majority. Post- and a-millennialists would be much less apt to do this, though non-premillennialist Louis Berkhof concedes that the *conjunction* of the signs would be of significance.

Is it possible to view the return apart from millennial con siderations? Theoretically—and perhaps ideally—yes. Neither Paul nor the synoptic writers mention the thousand years. In a way the millennial question adds complexity to the whole issue of Christ's coming again. But on the other hand, if the doctrine of a thousand year reign of Christ is truly biblical— and the Book of Revelation is surely part of the Bible—then it cannot be ignored in any major doctrinal formulation. Perhaps the best strategy would be to construct our doctrine of the return from the primary sources—Paul and the Synoptics—and then relate millennial conclusions to it.

WHAT ABOUT THE ANTICHRIST?

A kind of footnote to the millennial question is the issue

of *antichrist*. In a controversial passage Paul speaks of the coming of a "man of lawlessness," an enemy of Christ who opposes every object of worship "and takes his seat in the temple of God, proclaiming himself to be God" (2 Thess. 2:1-2). In John's letters the author warns against antichrists: "As you have heard that antichrist is coming, so now many antichrists have come" (1 John 2:18). Emil Brunner sees the concept of antichrist as the antithesis of millennium. Just as certain teachings of Jesus can be quoted in support of millennium as a symbol of progress (e.g., the parables of the mustard seed and the leaven), so can others be quoted for antichrist, its counterpoise (the parable of the wheat and the tares). The modern man of progress can become antichrist by his achievement of technical power and domination of men's minds (Could subliminal advertising be an example?). Brunner sees the two symbols of millennium and antichrist standing against each other in mutual limitation.[20] Thus we are permitted neither a superficial optimism nor a groveling pessimism about history. There is hope for human progress, but it is always limited by the reality of evil, both in man and around him.

IN SUMMARY

This seems a good time to share some personal impressions about the millennial issue. My first observation is that no one view can claim to be the whole truth. What seems to be valid scriptural support can be given for all three positions. While to each of us one view will doubtless seem better than the others, the biblical truth implied in the divergent views must be incorporated into the one we choose to support. A second impression is that since the Millennium is at best a difficult subject, it should never be made the touchstone of orthodoxy or Christian devotion, nor should it become the center of any personal or group theological position. The golden rule of biblical interpretation would seem to be: Start with the clear, unambiguous passages; learn well the lessons they teach; and

only then turn to the Scriptures that for whatever reason seem unclear and thus debatable (religious cults usually do the opposite, starting with the unclear and then making everything else conform to it). A third reflection is of a historical nature: the idea of the Millennium has given rise to many perfectionist societies, in both Europe and America. A few of these have lasted into our time, and some have become increasingly secular (such as the Amana community). But history would seem to testify to the power latent in the millennial idea. It is a concept we cannot ignore.

The Church and the Second Coming — Cults and Neglect

In chapter one we saw the doctrine of the return in the Bible. But it is also important to know what use was made of this in the ongoing life of the church. Was it ignored, or overemphasized? Did some people twist the doctrine into shapes that would be unrecognizable to biblical writers, or was it kept largely in its biblical form? Did some people go to the extreme of setting dates for the Great Day? The answer to each question is both Yes and No, depending on which time period one is talking about.

MONTANISM

The early church between the end of the apostolic age (100 A.D.) and Constantine (314) forms a manageable unit of study. The Christianity of the second century was becoming more and more formal and ecclesiastical. Christ's promise of his return was largely forgotten or at least subordinated to other interests. But truth, like compressed steam, is likely to make itself known, sometimes in violent and unpleasant ways. Such was the case

with a movement that arose in Asia Minor at mid-century. Led by a "prophet" (Montanus) and two prophetesses, it is known to church history as Montanism. To put the matter somewhat loosely, Montanism was the charismatic movement of the second century. Like the contemporary charismatic movement, it arose in reaction to a strong emphasis on ecclesiastical form. (Should it surprise us that the modern movement arose and continues to be centered in the most liturgical and formalistic churches?) Its major emphases were the Second Coming of Christ and vital dependence on the Holy Spirit.

As a movement to restore certain emphases of the apostolic church, Montanism should probably be applauded. But as so often happens, the restorers went too far. Before it was all over, the reformers needed reformation. They tried, and partly succeeded, in reproducing some features of the first century church. Unfortunately, they imitated the earlier church more in its vices than in its virtues, more in its mistakes than in its positive accomplishments. Their emphasis on individual revelation by the Holy Spirit introduced a subjectivism that was subversive of all faith. And in their understanding of the return they remind us of those Thessalonians who literally sat and waited for Christ, and of whom Paul had to say, "Shun any brother who is loafing" (2 Thess. 3:6, MOFFATT). Abandoning homes and occupations, they waited for Christ to set up his millennial kingdom in a small Asia Minor town. Their twisted doctrine of the return also led to a distorted ethic. They demanded a strict asceticism (although, unlike typical early Christian asceticisms, it was based on the imminence of the return, rather than a gnostic dualism of body and soul). Montanism was (rightly, I think) adjudged a heresy by the main body of the church.

Montanism can also serve as an example of something we see often in church history—the influence of a heresy upon the main body of the church. Professor Latourette lists Montanism's influence thus:

(1) The belief that the age of prophecy closed with the apostles.

(2) Distrust of teachers who claimed direct inspiration, but were not appointed by the bishop.

(3) The exaltation of episcopacy over prophets.

(4) More emphasis on the formation of the New Testament canon.

(5) A coolness toward any proclamation of the Second Coming.[21]

The first three have mixed value. For practical reasons it was probably good to draw a kind of line separating the apostolic and post-apostolic ages; but this should not be taken as excluding the continuing work of the Holy Spirit. More emphasis on the formation of New Testament canon had a positive benefit. Heresies such as Montanism forced the church to gather the books of the New Testament (Surprisingly, this process was not completed—to our knowledge—until about the middle of the fourth century). But the last result, that of producing coolness toward the Second Coming, was disastrous. For many centuries after, and up to the present day, Christians often gave only minimal attention to the return, for they would look back at the Montanists or other extremists and say, "That's what happens when you talk about the Second Coming!" We hope this book may help people see that such an attitude is bad logic and even worse theology!

NEGLECT OF THE SECOND COMING

The history of the doctrine for the next millennium-and-a-half is mainly one of sheer neglect, along with some abuse. St. Augustine (430 A.D.) was an anti-millenarian, and his enormous influence effectively silenced any who might otherwise have spoken. Or to put the matter more theologically—and charitably—perhaps God had other lessons he needed to teach the church in its development; the human mind can bear only so much at one time. In the Middle Ages the only one

worthy of mention was Joachim of Flora (1202 A.D.) who divided history into the ages of the Father, Son and Spirit, and taught that the age of the Spirit would begin in 1260 A.D.. Although having some similarities to millennarian views, his teaching was about the coming of the Spirit rather than of Christ. Even Luther and Calvin did not especially emphasize the return, though like Augustine and other Christian thinkers before them they believed the doctrine as part of the creed.

ANABAPTISTS

The next major example of emphasis on the return was among the Anabaptists of the Reformation period. Often called the "left-wing," or fourth phase of the Reformation (along with Lutheranism, Calvinism, and Anglicanism), the Anabaptists (literally the "re-baptized") tried to return to the Christianity of the first century. Critical of Roman Catholic practices, they were also unhappy with the Protestant reformers for their continued acceptance of doctrines such as infant baptism and support of the secular state. One could say rather loosely that they were somewhat similar to the Montanists in their desire to restore primitive Christianity, but most of them were much more temperate and less extremist-prone than the earlier group. In general, their stock is high now in the scholarly world. They were a serious, sincere group of people, many of whose ideas such as non-violence and religious toleration were ahead of their time and are now commonly accepted by most Christians.

However, one episode gave a bad name to the movement. An early leader, Melchior Hoffman, predicted that after his death he would return with Christ in the heavens and establish the new Jerusalem. Other extreme Anabaptist leaders believed that kingdom would be established in the German city of Munster. In February, 1534, they managed to take control of the city, and tried to establish a Christian society. A noble experiment, perhaps, but doomed to failure by extremism, such

as the instituting of polygamy and a community of goods (sometimes imprecisely called "Christian communism"). In June, 1535, an army composed of Catholic and Protestant forces captured the city. There were also other instances, though less dramatic, of apocalyptic extremism among the Anabaptists.

SEVENTH DAY ADVENTISTS AND JEHOVAH'S WITNESSES

A final illustration of earlier extremism forms a fascinating segment of American religious and cultural history. Interest in the return was high in nineteenth century America. In the fourth decade it finally took the form of date-setting. An upstate New York farmer, William Miller, intently studied Daniel and Revelation, and on the basis of mathematical computations from these books concluded that Christ would come in 1843. His followers were naturally disappointed that he was wrong, but they were reassured when he restudied the data and concluded that he had made a mistake of one year, and that Christ would come in 1844. When events proved him wrong a second time, Miller (to his credit) gave up the whole thing. But his followers were not so easily untracked. Under the eventual leadership of Ellen Harmon White they stayed together, forming what we now know as the Seventh-Day Adventist Church. Also, in the 1870s the Jehovah's Witnesses were organized by a group of "Millerites."

RECENT CULTS

Recent history also provides examples of millenarian apocalyptic enthusiasm. In the tempestuous late sixties, religious groups arose, especially among young people, that would be labeled "radical" by many Christians, Some of these, including the "Jesus people," were largely protest groups fueled in part by the anti-Vietnam sentiment that was so strong at the time. Also involved were the various liberation

movements—black, feminist, Third World, and others. Typically the movements related to the Jesus people put considerable stress on the Second Coming.

One group that has become well-known is the Children of God. Drawing largely from the Jesus people, they formed a movement that generated considerable heat, if not light. Specializing in Jeremiah-type prophecies of doom (the "doom boom," as one magazine calls it), they are not at all hesitant about making their message known, as in a famous cathedral in San Francisco, where they sat ominously silent during a service, and then at the end in one voice shouted, "Repent!" They vigorously encourage young people to drop out of the present world-system, join a children of God commune, and help prepare for the coming of Christ. By doing so they claim to escape the mark of the Beast, which will be put on all compromising Christians. For them the Great Tribulation is nearly upon us and afterward Jesus will return to establish his kingdom.

WHY HERESIES?

The history of heresies, such as we have seen, may seem like a negative and even depressing subject, the pathology of Christian doctrine. Actually it can have a positive and educational value. For we must ask ourselves: Why does a heresy arise? The discovery of an answer may prevent its recurrence, as well as provide some valuable lessons. In general, heresies and cults seem to arise because of a failure to present a full, well-rounded statement of Christian belief—a sort of spiritual vitamin deficiency to which the (ecclesiastical) body reacts. If we fail to stress the biblical teaching about health and healing, then healing cults arise. If we neglect the Bible's word on death and life everlasting, people turn to spiritism. And if we ignore the return of Christ, cults will arise that try to make up for that omission.[22] A cult or heresy is usually not so much fundamentally wrong as guilty of misplaced emphasis. To be heretical

is to take a part of the truth and make it seem to be the whole truth. Perhaps we should also extend the term to those who simply ignore an important part of the truth as many have done with the biblical teaching on the return.

Part Three

"Therefore, we must always be ready for him."

—C. S. Lewis, *The World's Last Night*

How Does the Second Coming Affect Me?

SPIRITUAL READINESS

The third and briefest section of this book is like a conclusion to a process of reasoning. "Christ will surely return" is the opening and major premise. "But we cannot possibly know when" is the second statement, continuing but clarifying the first. The third and final affirmation seems inevitable. If he will most certainly come, but has given us no exact indication of when, we must be ready at any time for that coming. If we know that Uncle John is coming to visit, we had better dust the furniture daily and have a room prepared—especially if he has told us that he does not know exactly when he will come. Lewis's own illustration is of a young scholar who comes to class unsure whether or not he will be called on to recite. But he had better be ready!

Personal Salvation

The most obvious way to be prepared for his coming is to be sure that we ourselves are Christians. Many people have

an appreciation for Christian truth and a general acceptance of Christian values, without a personal commitment to Christ. To draw an illustration from the contemporary social scene, it is comparable to people who are "living together" without having made a marriage commitment. There are people who are *friendly* to Christ and what he represents who have not pledged their lives to him. Let them do so now!

Right Living

A close second to being Christians ourselves is living the kind of life he desires of us. "If we love him, why not serve him?" asks the old spiritual. And one major way we serve him is concretely to show the world the Christian way of life. The church is sometimes described as "the extension of the Incarnation." The ecclesiastical implications of this may be disturbing to some (including the author), but its meaning for Christian living can hardly be denied. At the opening of the Book of Acts the author says that "in the first book" (the gospel of Luke) "I have dealt with all that Jesus began to do and teach." The word "began" is very interesting. The implication is that what he "began" has not yet been finished, and that in fact the church is completing or at least furthering what he commenced! Jesus is no longer physically in the world, but his church is. In theory—though unfortunately not always in practice—one should be able to see Christ in his church.

Reference has been made earlier to the ethical implications of his return, but we would do well to re-emphasize it here. We have not only the general Christian ethical obligation to urge us to right living ("live this way because Christ died for you") but also the eschatological motivation ("live this way because he may come at any moment"). Let us be thinking, speaking, imagining, desiring, planning, contemplating, doing—what we will want to be doing when Jesus comes.

Motivation for Evangelism

Another way to prepare for his coming is evangelism, the

sharing of the Good News with those both near and far—or, to use a currently popular description, one beggar telling another where to find bread. If being Christians ourselves is the first step in this preparation, surely helping others to be Christians must also have high priority. Some see this as actually hastening the return, for did not our Lord say, "This gospel of the kingdom will be preached to the whole world, as a testimony to the nations; and then the end will come"? (Matt. 24:14; also Mark 13:13) Charles R. Erdman, in an older but still useful book, sees the evangelization of the world as "the supreme precedent condition of his return," and then concludes, "Those who most eagerly look for the return of their Lord will be most earnest in pressing for the accomplishment of this task."[23]

Apart from the question whether we can hasten the return through evangelism, a simple spiritual humanitarianism should prompt us to share the message with as many as possible, as quickly as possible. Like the four lepers of Samaria who discovered a great store of food in time of starvation, but were tempted to keep it for themselves, we will say, "We do not well; this is a day of good tidings, and we hold our peace" (2 Kings 7:9 KJV). We will feel the force of Paul's anguished words as he says, "It is because of this solemn fear of the Lord . . . that we work so hard to win others" (2 Cor. 5:11 TLB).

Worship

Nowhere is the return of Christ more neglected than in worship services. Many typical churchgoers have probably never heard a sermon on the subject or more than a passing reference to the event. But there are several ways a conscientious worship leader can call attention to the doctrine. One is the use of hymns. Those churches with services of a more informal type will find numerous gospel hymns emphasizing the return. Some of these, such as "What If It Were Today?" and "Glad Day, Glad Day, Is It the Crowning Day?" have the return of

Christ as their sole theme. Others have the eschatological as one among several themes. Such a hymn is "One Day," which covers some of the major items of Christian theology, starting with the Virgin Birth, and in the succeeding stanzas dealing with the death, entombment, resurrection/ascension and return of Christ. A favorite of many is the Sankey gospel-hymn with the recurring lines:

> There'll be no dark valley when Jesus comes
> To gather his loved ones home.

The more traditional hymns are also not lacking in end-of-time references. A few of the classical hymns center on this theme. One of the most familiar is Charles Wesley's "Lo! He Comes with Clouds Descending." In others the Second Coming is implied. "Jesus Shall Reign Where'er the Sun," Isaac Watts' paraphrase of Psalm 72, makes little sense if it does not culminate in the ultimate kingdom of God; the phrase, "His Kingdom (shall) spread from shore to shore" has implications well beyond the Baby in the manger or the Teacher and Healer of Galilee.

The Lord's Supper also makes its unique contribution through the worship service. In Paul's classical explanation of the sacrament (1 Cor. 11:17-33) the Supper is presented in its varied temporal references. "As often as you eat this bread and drink this cup, you proclaim the Lord's death until he comes" (1 Cor. 11:26). The first half of the verse, before the comma, refers to the (Corinthian) present, the Sunday-by-Sunday experience of Christ's sacramental presence in the elements. The words immediately after the comma point to the past, "the Lord's death" upon the cross at Golgotha. The last three words are of special interest in the context of our subject. We are told to remember the Lord's death "until he comes." Far from being an afterthought, these words are the climax of the verse, the cymbal-crash at the end of the *crescendo*. The Lord's Table of the past and present find full meaning only in the Table of the future.

In addition to the general worship service with its eschatological implications, there could also be a special service devoted soley to this theme. Such an occasion would of course include appropriate hymns, Scripture readings and sermon. It might also feature a special litany. While many of those who "love his appearing" might not be liturgically inclined, they could surely find no fault in a liturgical celebration of the return. The following is submitted as at least a faltering step in this direction.

LITANY OF THE SECOND COMING

Pastor: *Father, through the prophets you promised that one day your Messiah would rule the world in justice and peace.*

People: Send that day to us soon, we pray.

Pastor: *You gave David to your ancient people as their King, and promised that from great David an even greater Son would come; and that he would take the throne which had been vacant so long.*

People: Thank you for Jesus Christ, the Son of David, and Your Son.

Pastor: *Through the prophets you told us of the Day of the Lord, a consummation of history in which both your judgment and your mercy will be manifest. In pride your people sometimes thought that Day would mean* **our** *exaltation rather than yours.*

People: Help us to be ready for that Day, when it comes.

Pastor: *Through your Son Jesus you told us of the time He would come again, and of the signs that would precede His coming. And yet we cannot set dates, for His coming will be unexpected, like a thief in the night.*

People: Help us to keep a watchful eye on human events, and yet to remember always that if even Jesus Himself did not know the time of His coming, neither can we.

Pastor: *Through your servant Paul you told us that the trumpet would sound, and the dead and then the living would go to meet the Lord.*

People: May we always comfort one another with these words.

Pastor: *Through your servant John you told us that whoever has this hope of Christ's coming purifies himself, even as He is pure.*

People: Give us the ethical inspiration of Christ's Second Coming. May we always be doing, thinking and saying what we would not be ashamed of when Jesus comes.

Unison: Lord Jesus, may the fact of your Second Coming free us from the fears and tensions we so often have—fear of a past we cannot change, of the future, of death and the life to come. Teach us that amidst the uncertainties of life, the one thing we can be sure of is that Christ will come again. May we, like the church of the Apostles, live in expectation of your coming. May we ever be watchful, ready for His coming, for we do not know the day or the hour. Maranatha. Come, Lord Jesus.

Creeds and Confessions

In connection with preparation through worship, a word should perhaps be said about the use of creeds and confessions of faith. The use of a great creed such as the Apostles' or the Nicene, can be a thrilling experience, and may add significantly to the worship service. Most of the creeds have good general statements about the return of Christ, usually identifying it with judgment of "the quick and the dead." Unfortunately, the richness of the full-orbed biblical teaching concerning his coming is not given. In addition to the fact that recited creeds must of necessity be reasonably short, this is

probably due in the main to the revulsion of creed-makers, both ancient and modern, against extremist movements such as millenarianism.

But the nineteenth century, with its renewed interest in the subject, produced helpful creedal affirmations. For example, the faith statement of the Free-Will Baptists (1834, 1868) says, "The Lord Jesus, who ascended on high and sits at the right hand of God, will come again to close the gospel dispensation, glorify his saints, and judge the world."[24] And the Confession of the Evangelical Free Church of Geneva (1848) states: "We believe that in that day, the dead who are in Christ . . . and the faithful then living on the earth, all transformed through his power, will be taken up together into the clouds to meet him. . . ."[25] Let us then enjoy and profit from the assertions in the great ancient and modern creeds concerning the later coming of Christ, while at the same time hoping that creed-makers of the future will deal more adequately with the subject.

The Second Coming — Motivation to Serve

Another area in which the return should be a stimulus is social service. At first hearing this may seem contrary to both logic and experience. The second charge I will accept, though only provisionally. The first, however, I must reject as a *non sequitur*, a logical short circuit, a real "bummer." The doctrine of Christ's return is *not* an invitation to religious privatism, to building tabernacles on mountains and neglecting present responsibilities (Matt. 17:4). We have elsewhere (on 2 Peter) considered the view that the return has been delayed for greater evangelization. And is not Christian social service an evangelism of works rather than words? If we want to do all the "spiritual" good we can before he comes, shall we not also want to give all the cups of cold water—or better, of hot soup—in his name that our time will permit? If, as noted earlier, Paul tells the Thessalonians not to be lazy but to *work*

while waiting for the return (2 Thess. 3), let us be studying and waiting, evangelizing and waiting, working in society and waiting, as we look to his coming.

The second charge, mentioned above, is asserting that the compatibility of eschatological belief and social service is contrary to experience. This is probably true, but like racial prejudice or sexism it is something that can be overcome. We have so often, in America in particular, come to think in stereotypes that we see the gospeller on one side with his beliefs, including the Second Coming, and the "liberal" social actionist on the other; and never the twain shall meet! We have, I hope, reached the point in Christian history at which we realize these two aspects of the gospel to be a case of inclusive ("both . . . and") rather than exclusive (either . . . or, but not both") alternation. "These you ought to have done," said Jesus (in admittedly different circumstances), "without neglecting the others" (Matt. 23:23).

Belief in Christ's return, then, can free us to work for him in the area of Christian social service. Our attitude should not be, "Christ is going to come, so I will stress the spiritual and ignore the social aspect of the faith." Rather we should say, "Christ's coming is sure; therefore I am freed to serve him in the world." We shall "wait for his Son from heaven" (1 Thess. 1:10); but shall not become "loafers" (2 Thess. 3:6 Moffatt) in the process. We shall heed the Second Coming implications of Matthew's parables of the Ten Maidens and the Talents (Matt. 25:1-30), but shall likewise take seriously the immediately following parable of the judgment, in which giving "the cup of cold water" in Christ's name is seen as the criterion for the judging (Matt. 25:31-46).

One of the choice chapters in the New Testament is 2 Timothy 4. Set within a group of books (the Pastoral Epistles) whose authorship is questioned by some scholars, it would not on the surface seem to be a candidate for such a title. But the same savants who question the literary material surrounding

it usually agree that chapter 4 contains a genuine Pauline ele-ment. By any standard it is one of the most moving passages in the New Testament. Paul, the old soldier, has fought his last battle, and is ready for his farewell trip. In Nordic saga the old warrior would be speaking his last words, even as the funeral boat was being readied. "I have fought the good fight, I have finished the race, I have kept the faith. Henceforth there is laid up for me the crown of righteousness, which the Lord, the righteous judge, will award me on that day, and not only to me but also to all who love his appearing." Perhaps nothing more needs to be said. We love a rose because of its beauty and scent. We appreciate a Mozart symphony for its charm and power; and the Christian "loves his appearing" simply because that is what is natural for a Christian to do. Like Emer-son's rhodora, "his appearing" is an ultimate that needs no other justification. It is "its own excuse for being."

Why is the Philosophy of Christ's Return Important?

INTELLECTUAL PREPARATION

"Pardon me; did you say the return is a —*philosophical* issue?" This may be the reaction of many a reader to the title of this section. The return is usually thought of as a part of theology, and by its detractors as a major ingredient in the history of religious fanaticism. But what possible connection can it have with philosophy?

Epistemology

Considering the dozen or so specific areas that make up the subject matters of philosophy—logic, ethics, metaphysics, politics, etc.—we find several that are at least distantly relevant to the return. Epistemology, or theory of knowledge, is one. How do we know of the return: hearsay, opinion, sensory evidence, feeling, personal authority? Also, assuming its factuality, how will we know when the event occurs? Will it be a secret coming known only through intuitive processes, or a coming seen by the world?

Ethics

Ethics is another relevant subject. The ethical implications of the return are dealt with elsewhere in these pages. Suffice it to say at this point that if motivation is important to right living, one can hardly imagine a higher motivation than the consummation of history. And if a bit of levity be permitted, those who believe in a worldwide reign of Christ in the Millennium might profit from a study of political philosophy. (I still remember from my youth the pastor who suggested that the millennial Christ would doubtless appoint a Baptist as his Secretary of the Navy, since deep water would be involved!)

Logic

An area of greater importance is logic. There is a certain spiritual logic to Christ's return. H. H. Rowley, British Old Testament scholar, has put it well.

> I do not regard the belief in the Second Advent as a delusion of primitive Christianity, but as something which is inherent in the foundational Christian beliefs. I would deprecate all attempts to determine when it is to take place, or to define its manner, but it seems eminently reasonable to believe that if the kingdom of God is ever to be realized on earth Christ will have the manifestly supreme place of it.[26]

There is another logical aspect of Christ's return, found, surprisingly, in the domain of literary criticism. Professor Frank Kermode, in his book *The Sense of an Ending*, points out that every story has an ending, just as it has a beginning. Basing his work in part upon Nietzsche's theory of fictions and Vaihinger's "as-if" philosophy, he observes that in science we operate with such fictions as the "laws of nature" and the "complementarity" principle. They are useful and helpful, but ultimately fictitious. Likewise, the concepts of beginning and end are in their way fictions, but fictitious in their descriptive

aspects, *not* in the factuality of the events being described. A child may describe a happening in a very exaggerated and idiosyncratic way, but this does not negate the reality being explained. We imagine a clock to be saying *tick-tock*, though the clock, were it sentient, would doubtless be surprised. Applied to history, *tick* is beginning, *tock* is end, and the time between is the course of human events. Vis-a-vis the Bible, *tick* is creation and *tock* consummation. The various biblical descriptions of the utimate tock must always be read with an understanding of the metaphorical use of language, especially in the area of metaphysics and religion.

If what has been said is correct, then, there is a "logic of the end." Every story has its last chapter, every symphony its *coda*, every race its finish line. The concept of an end is reasonable; it is the *lack* of an end that would defy logic.

Philosophy of History

All of these are in varying degrees minor, however, compared to the one area of philosophy in which the return should be a critical item of discussion. That is the philosophy of history. Since some readers, even those with philosophical backgrounds, may not be familiar with this division of the subject, perhaps a word of explanation is in order. The philosophy of history may be called that philosophical discipline which asks the question: Is there meaning, pattern and purpose in history? Early philosophers did not generally deal explicitly with the question, in part because the concept of time or duration was not usually taken seriously. Being, not becoming, was their prime concern. St. Augustine was the first one usually credited with a philosophy or a theology of history. Occasional maverick thinkers (Joachim, Vico), dealt with it in succeeding centuries, but by and large it was neglected until relatively recent time. Though many philosophers would question whether there is any grist for the philosophical mill in the events and course of history, it is often the topic of the most lively philosophical discussion.

It has been said that any viable philosophy of history must have adequate explanation of the source, course and goal of history (Romans 11:36 has such a division). The *source* of history would be involved with the return perhaps in the sense that a river's beginning, as well as its destination, would be of interest to a geographer. If we believe that reality is in the process itself, and not just in this or that event within it— and such is surely the prevailing philosophical and theological sentiment today—then no account of the sweep of history will be complete that ignores origins. The *course* of history is likewise related to the goal. To refer again to the concept of process, the realization of the goal arises *out of* the process, it is usually assumed. Assumed, that is, in its religious applications, by those who follow a "prophetic eschatology," believing that there are causes in history which lead to effects (The Book of Amos is an excellent example). But it is not assumed by those who are instructed by the "apocalyptic eschatology" school, for there the *discontinuity* of goal and process is emphasized; that is to say, in this view goal may have nothing to do with course. Most biblical scholars would argue for the former position, though not denying the validity of the apocalytic insights.

In a book of this theme, however, it is obvious that the *goal* of history is the major focus of interest; it is here that the concept of Christ's return is especially relevant. Surely no investigation of the *denouement* of history can be complete—especially from a Christian perspective—without a serious consideration of the event that Christianity says will in some sense bring history to a close. The *parousia*-phobia that afflicts us so often cannot be allowed to dominate here.

First, a note about terms is necessary. The Greek word *telos* can be translated "end" or "goal." It is from this that we derive "teleology"—the belief that reality is purposeful or goal oriented. Also, interestingly, this is a form of the Greek word used in one of Jesus' sayings on the cross—"It is finished"

(John 19:30). It could best be translated not as just indicated but in a way that would convey the thought of *his purpose being accomplished* ("It is accomplished," says the Jerusalem Bible and N.E.B.; "All is done," says the Basic English N.T.). *Telos* is to be distinguished from the Latin *finis*, which simply means "termination," with no thought of purpose achieved.

It is interesting that the English word "end" conveys both ideas. But as Reinhold Niebuhr observes, *finis* is a threat to *telos*; meaninglessness tends to overcome meaning, and the absurd often outshouts the rational and the moral.[27] Surely the Christian affirmation of how history will end is in terms of *telos*, not *finis*. If God has initiated and guided history, it is reasonable to assume that he will preside at its consummation, and that the consummation—like the last minute of a close sporting event—will achieve what the Master Coach had in mind before and during the game.

Concepts of *telos* can be classified according to their view of its temporal nature. For some it means the culmination part of a process, with no intrusion from "outside." Anything that happens is from "within the system." For others it is an event from beyond, not necessarily unconnected with the spacio-temporal process, but nevertheless fundamentally different from it. Or to put it more technically, some are teleologies of immanence and some of transcendence.

Is the end simply the result of what has been put into the pot over a period of years, like a stew that is a mixture of both good and bad elements? Or is it more to be compared to a prefabricated roof of a building, lifted by crane and put on a structure that it was designed for but with which it has had nothing to do? Another analogy would be to think of the different ways we put swimming pools in our backyards. We may dig the hole and lay the concrete ourselves. When all the concrete has been put in, and all other necessary parts have been added, the pool is finished. Or we might order a hole dug of a very specific size, and have a preformed fiberglass bottom,

perhaps made hundreds of miles from the hole, laid in it. The former would illustrate a teleology of immanence ("from within the system"), the latter a teleology of transcendence ("from outside the system").

Aristotle

Aristotle is an example of one who held an immanent teleology. The broad outline of his metaphysical system is well known to most readers of philosophy. We start with a hierarchical universe in which everything is seen both for what it is (actuality) and for what it can become (potentiality), that is, for its contribution to the ascending scale of things (the breeze-blown grass that is a beautiful field of green to a tourist is potential meat to a Colorado or Texas cattle rancher). But this process cannot go on forever; there must be a *terminus ad quem*, a final point at which an ultimate actuality is reached, the apex of the reality pyramid toward which all the pyramidal lines have been moving.

This apex is Aristotle's god, or prime mover (or unmoved mover). Though structurally related to all the rest of the universe, to which it serves as goalpoint, this prime mover is cognitively unrelated to all that is below it. It exists (or subsists) in a super-Olympian state drawing everything toward it like a metaphysical magnet, but totally oblivious of all that is below it. Its activity is only of the highest nature, which we have already said is thought. Thus, the mover eternally thinks about thinking. Remote, detached, unrelated, irrelevant—all these terms are applicable to this metaphysical ultimate.

But, somewhat paradoxically, this "god," though unrelated, is still within the system. The thought of a "supernature" other than nature, a realm of the divine different in kind from space-time, a beyond transcending the real as we know it, is not present in the Stagirite's thought. Aristotle's mover may be remote from man, but it is within the same reality mode.

Aristotle thus represents one kind of teleology of immanence,

in this case a *rational* culmination of natural process. We shall now examine instances of immanent teleologies that involve something other than the rational.

John Scotus Erigena

The next example is a much neglected but great early medieval thinker, John Scotus Erigena. A lonely eminence between Augustine and Anselm, he tried to incorporate both Christian and Neoplatonic elements into his system. More specifically, he endeavored to make philosophical bedfellows of the Christian doctrine of creation and the Neoplatonic concept of emanation. This was, to say the least, unsuccessful. The most interesting of his teachings is of the method of the divine self expression, or the procession of creatures from the divine. In his essential nature God is the uncreated who creates. Out of this essential being comes the realm of exemplary causes, similar in meaning to Platonic ideas. These are "created" (in a certain sense of the term) and are also creative. Next in the procession is the world of creatures in the phenomenal or space-time world. These are created but not creating. And last in the Neoplatonic procession is the end or goal, nature which is uncreated and uncreating, in which all things return into God, and ultimate reconciliation of all is achieved.

It is obvious that such a scheme, though interesting and thoughtful, is far more Neoplatonic than Christian, and is a hopeless weaving of incompatible philosophical skeins. It tries to combine the essentially transcendent with radical immanence; the result is quasi-pantheism with a Christian veneer. It represents a teleology of immanence, in this case with a *mystical* culmination of the process: the *telos* is the mystical absorption of all into God.

Under teleologies of immanence we have seen both a rational (Aristotle) and a mystical (Erigena) culmination. We now proceed to a third and modern type.

Pierre Tielhard de Chardin

Pierre Teilhard de Chardin represents a view of Christ's return that is difficult to classify. One's first reaction is probably to regard him as a kind of naturalistic postmillennialist; that is, for him the kingdom (or Omega Point) is to come through the evolution of resident forces until mankind, having reached the point of maximum maturation, is ready for the kingdom. Such a view might be considered naturalism with a Christian veneer, a kind of religious "process" philosophy. But further study may show that this is not quite the whole story. The Second Coming seems to be for him no mere linguistic accommodation to Christian tradition, but in a sense the keystone of his whole system. His philosophy views mankind as pressing toward the Omega Point, which, we are ultimately told, is Christ. Two forces are at work in man's development: the Forward impulse (progress) and the Upward impulse (worship and adoration). They will come together, he says, at the Second Coming. The present universe will not be destroyed but transformed. As for the time of the return, it will be like the First Advent—"in the fullness of time."

There is much that is refreshingly different in such a view. Its author is to be commended, I think, for endeavoring to bring together man's side and God's—the forward and the upward—though many feel that he overstresses the former. And the idea of the transformation of the universe at the *parousia* strikes an emotionally satisfying chord, reminding one of the teachings of the early Greek fathers. But there nevertheless remains a quasi-pantheistic and naturalistic substratum to his thought. His early statement that "the extraordinary adventure of the world will have ended in the bosom of a tranquil ocean" hardly reassures those disturbed about a possible pantheism, though he immediately explains that in this ocean "every drop will still be conscious of being itself."[28] For all its attractiveness his view seems to regard Christ's return as in some sense the end of a process—one in which God has been

at work, to be sure, but which is fundamentally natural. It may be regarded—not unfairly, it is hoped—as a pudding made from the recipe of Whitehead's process philosophy, with a dash of Christian theism on the top.

We have seen three instances of teleologies of immanence, in which the *telos* was seen as culminating in reason, in mystical experience and in providentially-guided natural process. In terms of the swimming-pool analogy, this teleology sees the pool as made from more or less local products. We dig the hole, pour the concrete and put in all the fixtures; we make the pool out of materials already at hand. Everything is from "within the system." Elements of this view may be seen in a popular hymn:

> Rise up, O men of God,
> His kingdom tarries long;
> Bring in the day of brotherhood,
> And end the night of wrong.

Very different, however, is the teleology that sees Christ's return as from "outside the system." Here, to continue our analogy, the pool is made of a one-piece fiberglass frame that is lowered by crane into a pre-existing excavation. It is not made of local materials but of something imported—or, to use the theological term—transcendent. However, this is of a qualified nature. *It is a transcendence that is not unrelated to the world.* To return to the swimming pool frame, it comes from the outside and is fashioned of materials not locally made, but *it must fit the contour of the excavation.* Thus though it is from the outside it is related to the local scene.

This may clarify the situation vis-a-vis the distinction already made between prophetic and apocalyptic eschatologies. Elements of both are involved in the New Testament view of the return: Christ's coming will be from the "outside" (apocalyptic), but is still related to the movement of history (prophetic).

Emil Brunner

The teleology of transcendence represents the basic or "mainstream" position of Christianity. Rather than examining it historically, which would be tedious, let us look at a recent theologian who epitomizes present Christian thought on the subject. With his usual clarity and conciseness, and with the faithfulness to biblical teaching characteristic especially of his later work, Emil Brunner well states the case.

In his book *The Christian Doctrine of the Church, Faith and the Consummation*, Brunner argues that God's coming to man is the dominant message of the Bible—not just one theme among many, but "*the one* theme that dominates everything else." The essence of the biblical story is captured in the three simple phrases, "He has come, He is here, He will come." Take away any one, he says, and you destroy the whole. Brunner is to be commended for his emphasis on the personal character of the biblical message. It is not only facts about God but God himself who is revealed. And He is not just the God of interstellar space, but One who comes to man at the parting of waters, at desert bushes, in Shiloan temples, at wedding feasts, on Damascus roads. Most Christians take seriously God's revelation in the Old Testament and in Christ ("He has come") and His spiritual presence today ("He is here"). When will we take with equal seriousness the fact that "He will come?"

Brunner also emphasizes what the present book hints at occasionally, that the character of the return as an event is unimaginable. The same, of course, can be said of most of the realities of "eschatology." The Bible speaks of heaven as having "streets of gold" and a tree that unceasingly bears fruit. Paul describes the return as initiated by the blowing of a trumpet; and Jesus says that at his coming two shall be working in a field or sleeping in a bed; one shall be taken and the other left. Taken literally, such word-pictures do not convey a consistent message, but they do not need to. Indeed, did not

Paul (quoting the Old Testament) say that "Eye has not seen, nor ear heard, what God has prepared for those who love him?" (1 Cor. 2:9) Perhaps we could paraphrase and say, "The imagination cannot conceive what God has in store for us."

True to his Neo-orthodox position, Brunner insists that only as an event from the "wholly other" can the return be the ultimate act of redemption and consummation. He would thus reject the thinkers already discussed as possessing teleologies of immanence. But the Zurich theologian somewhat qualifies his strong assertion of transcendence by saying that the return is not wholly other in relation to "the new being already begotten," or to "the Christ who is in us." This is consistent with what he has stated above; to say that "He will come" is not to deny that "He is here." Thus when Paul speaks of the mystical presence of Christ in the church, and when John implies that in a sense Christ has already come in the coming of the Spirit at Pentecost, there is not on the part of either any denial of a final, consummating return of our Lord.

Brunner is helpful also in his comments on the temporal aspect of the return. Some people agonize over the question: Precisely when will He return? Brunner observes that there is a kind of independence of faith from this chronological question, for, as Oscar Cullmann has shown, the saving event— the first coming of Christ—has already happened, and the return is thus not a wholly new event, but the second chapter of what has already begun. It is as if a prestigious person whom we had already met were returning to visit us. The anxiety and concern we might have felt at the initial visit would be dissipated, for now we would already know the visitor. The important fact would be the assurance of the return visit; the timing would be of secondary importance.

Most interestingly, Brunner sees a connection between vitality of faith and belief in the return. It is "something like a law," he says, that "the more powerfully life in the Spirit of God is present in the church, the more urgent is the expectation of the coming of Jesus Christ." Possession (of the Spirit)

and expectation (of the return) always go together, as in the earliest church. The present writer cannot but endorse the Swiss scholar's words. The vitality of the earliest church was always closely connected with its belief in the imminence of Christ's return. Conversely, the post-apostolic church lost both its fervent belief in the return and the vitality of its faith. That the Montanists of the later Second Century became fanatics on both points is no refutation. As stated earlier, *abusus non tollit usum*; abuse does not destroy legitimate use.

Finally, Brunner is very much aware of the overarching importance of the return. No trivial or secondary teaching, this; rather is it the keystone of the doctrinal arch. Without the return, Christianity is "a check that is never cashed," "a flight of stairs that leads nowhere."[29] Few recent theologians of world reputation have spoken more positively of "the blessed hope."

HOW DOES THE PHILOSOPHY OF CHRIST'S RETURN AFFECT THE WORLD?

What then can be said in retrospect about the return as a part of the philosophy of history? One of the most obvious conclusions is that the return, if viewed as factual, lays low the myth of "eternal recurrence" or inevitable historical cycles. There can be no cycles if history is ended. From a Christian perspective it is wrong in at least two respects. Its doctrine of the inevitable takes away any real responsibility from the individual, for how can we hold people accountable for what is eternally decreed? And worse, it leaves no room for radical newness and uniqueness in history—a point St. Augustine made so well in his *City of God*. It rules out the "once-for-all" quality of Christian faith—a unique Incarnation, a non-comparable Resurrection. Far from being a cyclical or circular view of history, Christianity is a linear view; a line that moves arrowlike from creation to consummation. The return is thus the ultimate confirmation of the biblical understanding of history.

Another emerging conclusion is the Christocentric nature of our faith. The Christian view of history is obviously theistic or God-centered. But the same could be said of most of the world's other religions. The uniqueness of the Christian view is that it is *Christ*-centered (Schweitzer similarly speaks of the difference between an amorphous God-mysticism, and a Christ-mysticism, which preserves the Creator-creature distinction).[30] The Old Testament, as the early Bonhoeffer reminds us, is at its deepest level the Book of Christ. What the Old Testament is *implicitly*, the New Testament is *explicitly*; witness the "theology of geography" in such places of Christ's life as Bethlehem, Nazareth, Cana, Sychar, Capernaum, Olivet, Calvary (each place suggests a doctrine related to Christ or an event implying such a doctrine). How fitting that the historical line end with the return of the Christ in whom all the story is focused. He is Alpha and Omega, Beginning and End; and Center also, as represented by the Cross and Resurrection.

Evolution and the Return of Christ

The concept of the return of Christ is also a rebuff to the "automatic progress" school of historical thought. It has sometimes been said that the theory of evolution and the return are incompatible. Perhaps so, but not in the way one might think. We must distinguish between evolution as (1) a theory of biology and (2) a basis for social philosophy (or what C. S. Lewis calls "the Great Myth"). It is difficult to see how evolution in sense number one is necessarily at odds with our doctrine. Some would argue that the scientific theory is in conflict with the Christian view of creation; that is a matter of debate. But Christ's return is certainly a blow to social Darwinism, which views biological evolution as a basis for social evolution. All our plans for "the Great Society," for the New, Fair, or Square Deals must take account of the possibility of their abrupt termination. "Two shall be in the

field" (for us, read factory, classroom, gymnasium or even church service); "one shall be taken, and the other left." The return is the ultimate cut-off, the final cessation of "progress." Progress there will be, but by God's action, not man's, and in ways more suggestive of revolution than of evolution.

We have come to the point at which a very basic issue needs to be addressed, a subject that to some will seem self-evident, but to others will be a matter of intense debate. This is the question: Will the return be a matter of history, a datable, verifiable, public event, not one that is done "in a corner?" (Acts 26:26) Or will it rather be an event of metahistory (whatever that means), a subjective appearance of a sort, a variety of contemporary Damascus-road experience, but not an objective, space-time event amenable to sensory investigation?

OTHER PHILOSOPHIES OF THE SECOND COMING

Various positions have been taken by those who reject the concept of a final, objective, end-of-time return of Christ. One of these is the view that Christ returned in the coming of the Spirit, a view sometimes said to be taken by the gospel of John. There is probably a measure of truth here. In contrast to the first three gospels, one finds relatively little in John about an end-of-history return of Christ. Rather Jesus promises the coming of the Spirit, saying that when the Spirit comes "He will glorify me, for he will take what is mine and declare it unto you" (John 16:14). The Book of Acts also affirms the close connection between Christ and the Spirit when it speaks of the Holy Spirit as "the spirit of Jesus" (Acts 16:7). Similar language can also be found in Paul (Rom. 8:2). John may seem to be saying, in effect, "You people who are wondering why Christ has not yet returned, take heart! In a sense he has returned—in the coming of the Spirit" (a position more apt to be taken by those who theologically reinterpret the gospel than by the fraternity of New Testament scholars). There is

probably nothing wrong with such an understanding as long as it does not obscure the truth of an ultimate return of Christ. The "coming" of Christ in the Holy Spirit may be thought of as *a* return; but it must not displace *the* return.

Any discussion of the question of the nature of Christ's return must take account of the pioneering work of New Testament scholar C. H. Dodd. To put it briefly, Dodd, in his "realized eschatology," argues that when Jesus talks of the kingdom of God it is not—or at least, not primarily—a kingdom that is to come, but one that is already here (in his latest writing Professor Dodd did accept the reality of a future coming). It seems undeniable that the teaching of Jesus, especially in the parables—with the miracles as supporting evidence—contains such an element. The crucial question, however, is whether that is *all* Jesus meant by the kingdom. And the almost unanimous answer of contemporary New Testament scholars is negative. In the later Testament, they say, there is a healthy tension between the present and future aspects of the kingdom. It is present now, but not in fullness. That will occur in the eschatological future. The return of Christ, then, cannot be "spiritualized" away into some kind of present experience. Christ is present in our lives now; he will be present in an indescribably greater way at his return.

Closely related to the "realized eschatology" of the previous paragraph is the view that Christ "comes" to us in special moments of life—often in crises, sometimes in periods of spiritual exaltation, and in especially meaningful experiences in the body of Christ, such as Eucharist and baptism. Commenting on the next-to-last verse in the Bible ("Surely I am coming soon . . . Come, Lord Jesus"), Professor G. B. Caird observes that the prayer was answered each week as Christ revealed himself to them in the eucharistic fellowship. At a deeper level he sees in this prayer the petition that "Christ will come again to win in his faithful servant (that is, in that servant's experience of persecution) the victory which is both

Calvary and Armageddon.''[31] In this view Christ not only comes again, but again and again. As above, the view must be regarded as true: but the feeling persists that it is not the *whole* truth.

Another view sometimes held about the return, though more by lay people than by those technically trained in theological matters, is that Christ's return is synonymous with one's death. It is hard to know the origin of such an idea. Certainly there is little warrant for it in the New Testament, though neither could it be directly contradicted therein. It is probably more a matter of semantics and the use of language than of theology. If we are prepared to admit that there is a "coming" of Christ in the Eucharist, why could we not speak similarly of the experience of death? Indeed, on Catholic assumptions both experiences are, or can be, sacramental. But such language is confusing. Let us call a rose a rose (whatever its sweetness), a spade a spade, and a Second Coming a Second Coming.

Thus we are brought to the one remaining major option: that the return will be an objective, public, even datable event. Surely this is the clear import of the passages we have examined earlier in this book.

> "Two men will be in the field; one is taken and one is left" (Matt. 24:40); "This Jesus who was taken up from you into heaven will come in the same way as you saw him" (Acts 1:11); "The Lord himself will descend from heaven . . . then we who are alive, who are left, shall be caught up." (1 Thess. 4:16-17)

It is difficult to find subjectivity or esoteric experience in these words.

Of course we cannot know the exact nature of the return, in the sense that a journalist would describe a happening, or a scientist make a chemical analysis. But the return will be real, the New Testament is saying, so utterly real that its details are unimportant.

WHAT DOES IT MATTER?

And finally, let us state without equivocation that the doctrine of the return is a central, not tangential, part of the Christian worldview, especially of the philosophy of history. It is essence, not accident, as a medieval philosopher might have put it. It is the logical completion of the whole structure of Christian thought. Without it, Christianity is a dinner without dessert, a church without a steeple, a novel without a last chapter, an unfinished symphony.

This may help answer a question that frequently arises when the return is mentioned: "Very interesting, but if Christ does not come in my lifetime how does all this concern me? Why get excited about something I may have no direct part in?" Two responses come to mind. First, *all* of us will be concerned with the return, whether or not we are living when he comes again. When he returns, says Paul, "the dead in Christ will rise first," before "those who are alive and remain." So we shall all be involved.

The second comment is that the return is vital to us as a completion of the Christian worldview. *Whether or not Christ will come in our lifetime is not the issue here.* The issue, as in the time of Augustine, Anselm, Luther and Wesley—that is, in *any* period of Christian history—is the place of the return in the Christian thought structure. And the evidence presented in these pages suggests that this place is one of monumental importance.

In summary, we have been looking at the Return of Christ as a matter of philosophy, and especially the philosophy of history, which deals with the source, course and consummation of history. Christ's return is seen as the consummation or *telos* of history. We saw that basically there are two kinds of *telos*, from (1) within the system (that is, the universe), and (2) from outside or beyond the system. Various schools of immanent teleology (#1, of the previous sentence) were examined, none of which—in spite of certain strengths—were seen

as adequate. The author's view is that only a transcendental teleology (#2 above) is adequate, satisfactorily meeting both philosophical and biblical demands. But this is not to advocate an other-worldly position, for the Christ who is to come is already here, in his Spirit (the Holy Spirit).

CHAPTER 8

The Ultimate Liberation

After an objective analysis of the major issue relating to Christ's return, I feel that I owe it to the reader to speak personally and subjectively. To what kind of conclusion may one come after examining the many facets of our topic?

The first and most obvious conclusion is the certainty of his return. To the Christian, like anyone else, the future is a matter of uncertainty. Job, health, finances, family status, weather—all can at best be known only as probable. But this is not true of the Second Coming. Christ's return, to the Christian, is the one future event that is *not* uncertain. Just as surely as Christ "was crucified, dead and buried" and "the third day arose again from the dead," so shall he "come to judge the quick and the dead."

The return of Christ will be a time of great joy to the Christian. Paul tells the Thessalonians to "comfort one another with these words" about the return. The prayer, "Come, Lord Jesus" (Rev. 22:20), would not have been uttered had the author not wished it with all his being. While to the non-Christian the coming again of our Lord may be an event to

dread, it is not so to "those who love his appearing." It is such an expectation that led Sankey to write that "there'll be no dark valley when Jesus comes," "no more sorrow, but a glorious morrow, when Jesus comes." For it is the moment when the Bridegroom, though delayed, comes to claim his bride (Matt. 25:10). Who can be sad at such a time?

If Christ's return will bring joy in the future, so it does in the present. One cannot read the New Testament carefully without sensing the joy such a concept brought to the early Christians. I must believe that a large measure of the vitality, even the ecstacy, of that "first fine careless rapture" we call the apostolic church should be attributed to belief in the return. And, correspondingly, that a major explanation of the contrast between the vitality of the first and the lassitude of the second-century church lies in the lack of this emphasis in the latter. And further, I must believe that the contemporary church will not recover the rapture of the apostolic era until it rediscovers that period's vivid expectation of the Second Coming. There can be no true apostolic *kerygma* without *maranatha*.

I believe also that belief in the return will make a difference in my living. Far from being pie-in-the-sky, the return is meat on the table, ethically speaking. My need to be ready for Christ's coming will make a difference in the words I speak, in the ideas I contemplate, in the things I do. The doctrine will affect both my personal deeds and my actions in society, for if there is good that needs to be done before Christ comes, whether on personal or social levels, let it be done! I will ponder the truth of what John says in his letter, that "everyone who has this hope in him purifies himself."

Having said all the foregoing, I must add that the return, like any other Christian doctrine, must take its place in the full-orbed circle of Christian beliefs. It is a great and basic doctrine, but must not be made to overshadow other equally important tenets of the faith, such as the Trinity, Incarnation,

Atonement, and Providence. When it is made the central doctrine of the faith it distorts the total picture, giving rise to cults or sects. It is only in the context of Christian theology as a whole that the return has meaning. So I will emphasize the doctrine, as a great and precious part of my faith, but I will not overemphasize it.

And finally, I cannot but believe that belief in Christ's return is the ultimate in liberation—female and male. All our "planning" for the future—ourselves, the church, and society—all our talk about spiritual development, cultivation of ecclesiastical graces, formation of a Christian lifestyle, must reckon with the possibility that the one who comes "like a thief in the night" may cut short all our plans. Like the rich man in Jesus' story, we may build larger barns (in our century, read libraries, computer memory banks, nuclear missile systems), only to hear the stern word, "This night your soul is required of you." Thus we know that the meaning of life for Christians is not to be assessed in terms of committee membership, program planning or the hundred other areas in which they might be involved, but ultimately in their readiness to meet the Savior at his coming. We are commissioned to tend the palace for the King while he is away, but we recognize that when he returns all our work —important as it is—is superseded by a higher reality and thus rendered obsolete. The certainty of Christ's return, then, enables us to assess our true priorities. When the Bridegroom comes we cease to worry about the details of the wedding; these are lost in the wonder of his person. The coming of the King-Bridegroom is what finally matters. This is the ultimate liberation!

Epilogue

The Once and Future King (A Christmas Sermon)

We have just come through the days of the Christmas season. Falling snow, lighted Christmas trees, Yule decorations, children in toy departments, street-corner Santas, Salvation Army lassies with their tinkling bells—all attested to the reality of the holiday season. And what is true in the secular is even more evident in the churches. Typical of the difference between this and the rest of the year are the hymns used in our Advent services. Instead of "Onward, Christian Soldiers" we sing about the birth of the Prince of Peace; we celebrate the "Three Kings of Orient" making their way to the holy Child rather than joining in "O Worship the King." We have been in the Advent season, which the popular song reminds us is "the most wonderful time of the year."

But the word Advent has another usage in the Christian vocabulary. It refers not only to the coming of Christ at Bethlehem but also, when we add the word "second," to his coming at the end of history. The first Advent celebrates his coming in the weakness of infancy, the second, his return in

the power of royalty. The first is the suffering Christ, the second is Christ the conqueror. The first we associate with Bethlehem and Nazareth, the second with what Nazareth geographically overlooks—the plain of Armageddon and (whatever it may mean) a famous battle associated with it.

And I can't think of a better time than the Christmas season to talk about the Second Advent. This doctrine has traditionally been a kind of orphan in the family of Christian beliefs. We know it is there, but almost no one—except the extremists— has welcomed it into the home. We are in danger of losing it amidst the welter of special emphases, from Fathers' Day to Labor Day to United Nations Day. But here is a theme of unquestioned biblical character, one of the major topics of the New Testament. It seems to me most fitting to think about his Second Coming in connection with our celebration of his first coming. Let us consider, then, the two advents in their similarities and differences; or, to use W. L. White's title for King Arthur, the saga of "the once and future King."

Before we do this directly, however, we need to consider an important question relating to the philosophy of the advents. Are we to see them primarily in terms of continuity or discontinuity, of contrast or similarity? Are the two advents more comparable to a long river such as the Mississippi or Danube whose upper and lower parts are so different as to make us question that they have the same identity, or are they more like a lake whose ends are so similar as to be virtually indistinguishable? I suggest that a concept midway between should be our model. The New Testament seems to present some difference of emphasis; Hebrews 9:28 is one of many verses that could be cited here. But the two cannot be understood as fundamentally alien, for the angel tells the awe-struck disciples at the Ascension that "this *same* Jesus shall come in like manner as you have seen him go into heaven" (Acts 1:11 KJV, italics added). The Second Advent must be thought of as volume two of the Great Story: different from

volume one, to be sure, but with even the differences growing out of motifs implicit in the first volume.

One difference between the two advents is the *main emphasis* or *theme* of each. A good biblical passage on which to base our thinking here is Luke 4:16-30. This Scripture tells of Jesus returning to his hometown, Nazareth, and speaking in the synagogue. Reading from Isaiah 61, Jesus spoke these words to the worshippers:

> The Spirit of the Lord is upon me,
> because he has anointed me to preach
> good news to the poor.
> He has sent me to proclaim release to the captive
> and recovery of sight to the blind,
> to set at liberty those who are oppressed
> to proclaim the acceptable year of the Lord.

Much has been made of the significance of this incident. Some see in it a kind of encapsulated account of the whole life and ministry of Jesus. One scholar (G. A. Smith) finds in the Isaiah passage the origin of the New Testament word *gospel* ("good news"). It is no doubt of significance that Jesus, according to Luke, omits the phrase, "the day of vengeance of our God," which in Isaiah 61 immediately follows the phrase, "to proclaim the acceptable year of the Lord." Whether or not the Old Testament writer meant to make a sharp distinction between the "acceptable year of the Lord" and the "day of vengeance" may be a matter of debate; but Jesus' omission of the phrase shows the major motif of his ministry. Some present-day Christians would see—perhaps too simply—the "acceptable year of the Lord" as a reference to the first coming of Christ, and the "day of vengeance" as describing the Second Advent. While there may be some truth to such a distinction, mainly as a matter of emphasis, it seems better to regard both phrases as applying to each coming, lest we too sharply separate the characters of the two advents, and forget that it is "this same Jesus" (Acts 1:11) who will come again.

Perhaps it will be helpful to look at a related concept, the relationship of the Old and New Covenants. It is a theological commonplace to say that the Old or Mosaic Covenant, given at Sinai, has been superseded by the New, which was announced by Jeremiah (Jer. 31:31-34), and affirmed by Jesus (Mark 41:24 and parallels), Paul (2 Cor. 3) and the author of Hebrews (Heb. 8). One of the most important questions a biblical theologian can ask is: What is the relationship between the covenants? Indeed, much of one's understanding of the Bible rests on the answer to this question.

Various alternatives can be quickly surveyed. One extreme is the answer of the *complete equality* of the covenants, or testaments (we shall use the word "covenant"). This ignores the elements of historical development and (if I dare use a sometimes abused term) the progress of revelation; obviously the command to apply the rule "an eye for an eye" (Ex. 21) has not the same authority for us as the ethical imperatives of the Sermon on the Mount. Another is the answer of *complete discontinuity*—that the two covenants have nothing to do with each other. This was the view of Marcion, second century heretic, who argued that the Old Testament is a corrupting influence which should be eliminated from the New. If Marcion was right, obviously, almost all other Christians have been wrong, including the apostles and Jesus himself.

Without trying to look at all possible opinions on the subject, we can state the view representing the best of contemporary Christian scholarship: the true relationship between Old and New Covenants is most adequately expressed by the words "promise" and "fulfillment." The Old Covenant anticipates the Christian gospel, and, in so doing, is itself a gospel; the New Covenant records and declares the events of that gospel. This partially brings together the two somewhat competing themes of equality and inequality: equality, in that the two covenants are part of the same plan; inequality, in that the later represents a more advanced phase of that plan.

By a kind of analogy, may not the same be said of the two advents? Each advent seems to be a completion of the period it concludes, and a pointing forward to the next epoch. If the theme of the Old Covenant is *preparation* or *promise*, then so must be that of the advent that concludes it. At the same time that advent is obviously *more* than just promise: it is fulfillment at a high level. But in that the fulfillment is but partial, it can still appropriately be called "promise." This is similar to our understanding of the kingdom of God, which is present now, but will be complete only in the eschatological future.

Correspondingly, if the motif of the New Covenant is *fulfillment* or *consummation*, that would likewise be the emphasis of its epoch-ending advent. Just as a symphonic work may have themes that are fragmentary in the early part but complete and triumphant in the conclusion, or as a novel or detective tale may have story-threads toward the beginning that are eventually woven into an impressive whole; so the motifs of the First Advent are restated and recapitulated—with trumpets—in the Second Advent.

In summary, then, we may speak of both advents as fulfillment, but one a lesser and the other a greater fulfillment. The First Advent, being the lesser, is also promise in that it points toward the greater. The advents may be regarded as similar; but it is a similarity "with a difference."

A second difference between the advents is in the *extent* of their immediate impact. The New Testament itself frequently speaks of the First Advent in diminutive rather than hyperbolic terms. Paul describes it as a time of humiliation (Phil. 2:8); Peter thinks of it in terms of suffering (1 Peter 2:21-25; 4:1); and the author of Hebrews characterizes it as a period in which Christ was "made lower than the angels" and became "perfect through suffering" (Heb. 2:5-10). The gospel of John regards the cross as a victory ("It is finished," that is, salvation has been achieved—John 19:30), but it is a victory achieved

through suffering. The Book of Revelation also sees the work of Christ as triumphant: Christ is the Victorious Lamb, whose praise the whole world sings; but his being the Lamb implies suffering and sacrifice. In general it can be said that the prevailing image of Christ in the New Testament is that of Suffering Servant (Isaiah 53), who gives himself to bear the sins of many.

The immediate impact of his first coming, then, was not great. In modern terms it was in no sense a "media event." People watching its details on the evening news during supper would have switched to another channel, so commonplace would have been the material covered. Cattle, children playing together, a carpenter shop, a man talking to people on a hillside, would bore us beyond measure; and a shot of the three crosses on the lonely hill would not help us digest our pie á la mode. To the people of Nazareth, Jesus was just a child from the carpenter's family ("Is not this Joseph's son?", Luke 4:22), one who surprised them when he achieved a measure of fame. And in the empire itself his name is found—outside Christian or Jewish historians—only in a few obscure lines in Tacitus and Pliny. In Anatole France's fictional story *The Procurator of Judea,* Pilate, in his retirement, could barely remember Jesus at all. Phillips Brooks was right when he described that advent by saying,

> "How silently, how silently, the wondrous Gift is given."

But in his Second Coming the scenario changes. Instead of lowing cattle there are high, piercing trumpets. The Gift is given, not in silence but amidst universal acknowledgment—whatever may be the motivation of that acknowledgment. Paul states the earliest Christian belief when he says to the Thessalonians:

> The Lord himself will descend from heaven with a cry of command, with the archangel's call, and with the sound of the trumpet of God.
>
> (1 Thess. 4:16)

Hardly a private audience with the King, that! The mind boggles at the thought of the media coverage that could be given to such an event, with communication satellites and worldwide television. But we would probably do well not to pursue that line of thought too avidly. For one thing, the coming will be sudden—"like a thief in the night," Jesus says; it is not an event involving a global press conference. And for another thing, we cannot deny the possibly symbolic character of the language. Such phrases as "a cry of command," "the archangel's call," and "the sound of the trumpet of God" should probably not be regarded as realities that can be measured in decibels! But Paul's point is clear enough: Christ's return will be public and universally known.

A further difference between the advents lies in *the role of human choice* implied by each. Christ's first coming was God's offer of life to the world. Many biblical passages support this, but perhaps the most eloquent is from the last book of the New Testament.

> The Spirit and the Bride say, "Come." And let him who
> hears say, "Come." And let him who is thirsty come,
> let him who desires take the water of life without price.
> (Rev. 22:17)

Some Christians may be troubled by a possible conflict between this concept and the idea of predestination. This is not the time to delve into the issue, except to state my earnest conviction that the *biblical* doctrine of predestination—as distinct from some theological additions—presents no irreconcilable difference. That the coming of Christ and his redemptive work constitute the "good news" or gospel, that this gospel is offered to the world now in sincerity and good faith, that people may accept that gospel and thereby enter into life—this is surely the meaning of the age in which we live, according to the New Testament.

The Second Coming, however, suggests a different emphasis.

"Two men will be in the field," says Jesus; "one is taken and one is left" (Matt. 24:40). The different actions obviously reflect the disparate religious commitments of the two. Paul's great paragraph on the subject in 1 Thessalonians, already mentioned, assumes that decision for Christ has already been made. "The dead in Christ," who will rise first, are the Christian dead; and "we who are alive, who are left" (1 Thess. 4:17) refers to those who have believed in Christ. It seems clear that the Second Coming is a time not when decision is sought but when the results of that decision are manifest.

A striking passage in 2 Peter, a late New Testament book, suggests that the reason for the delay in his coming—an important issue to people living several decades after his Incarnation—was to give us time to make our choice for Christ; "The Lord is . . . forbearing toward you, not wishing that any should perish, but that all should reach repentance" (2 Pet. 3:9). This emphasis is confirmed in a brilliant passage from C. S. Lewis:

> We can guess why He's delaying [his Return]. He wants to give us the chance of joining His side freely . . . When the author walks out on the stage, the play's over . . . It will be too late then [at the Return] to *choose* your side . . . This won't be the time for choosing; it will be the time when we discover which side we have really chosen, whether we have realized it before or not. *Now* is our chance to choose the right side. God is holding back to give us that chance. It won't last forever. We must take it or leave it.
>
> (*The Case for Christianity*, 55-56)

And so we come back to the title of the sermon, "The Once and Future King." In his First Advent he came to be king in a spiritual sense. He proclaimed this symbolically when he rode like a king into Jerusalem on the first Palm Sunday. No doubt the gospel writer had this in mind when he recorded Pilate's question, "Are you a King?" and Jesus' answer, "My kingship

is not of this world" (John 18:33-38). I trust we all realize that this kingship of Jesus is not just ancient history. Jesus offers himself to us—*today*—as our king. Sometimes we sing the hymn beginning, "King of my life, I crown thee now." I hope we believe what we sing.

His future kingship in relation to his present reign in our lives is what the Second Coming is all about. There are many details about it that we do not know—indeed, that we probably *could* not know because of the meta-historical nature of the events. This should not dim our expectation. If the return of Christ was the hope of the first century church, it is also our hope. If the earliest Christians found solace in this great concept, so can we—and so should we. In life's high moments and low, whether smiling or grimacing in pain, in times of "sweetness and light" as well as "storm and stress," we can echo the words of Sankey's hymn

"There'll be no dark valley when Jesus comes."

The One who is our King now will one day be our King in an even greater, almost unimaginable sense. "Hallelujah," says the Book of Revelation, "for the Lord God Omnipotent reigns." "Even so, come Lord Jesus."

Appendix

Sectarian Understandings of the Return

"End-Time" Writers

The Author's Choices

C. S. Lewis

"The Second Coming," by D. L. Moody

Sectarian Understandings
of the Return

When we think of the Second Coming or Advent of Christ, we may remember an organization, the Seventh-Day Adventist Church, which gets part of its name from this doctrine. At first glance one may think that this church (hereinafter to be called SDA) and dispensational premillennialism have much in common, but this is not necessarily so—at least, so the Adventists maintain. They believe Christ's coming is near but at a time "not disclosed," thus deviating from the older Millerite policy of setting dates. There will be only one coming of Christ (not two, as dispensational premillennialists teach) which will interrupt and terminate the Battle of Armageddon. The Millennium then begins, but it is a thousand years of desolation on earth, for the wicked have been exterminated and the saints raptured or taken up. Only Satan and his fallen angels inhabit it for that period. There are three resurrections: of the righteous, before the Millennium; of the wicked, after the Millennium; and a special resurrection, before the Second Advent, to include both unbelievers ("they who pierced him")

and SDA believers who died since 1846. In all candor, the latter part of this special resurrection, concerning the deceased SDA members, is more a deduction from various official pronouncements than a direct statement from Adventist leaders.

In general, the SDA position on Christ's return, while having its own special flavor, is not significantly different from general premillennial teaching; the difference is more in the method of advertising and presenting it (I will long remember an SDA television commercial, announcing a local series on the return, that featured pictures of great flames, presumably of hell).

But the Jehovah's Witnesses, who grew indirectly out of the SDA movement, deviate significantly from their Adventist predecessors. For them, Christ will return only in a symbolic, spiritual sense. In fact, he has already returned, in 1914, when he established his kingdom (hence the name "kingdom hall" for their place of worship). Rather than a true Second Coming, the Witnesses teach in effect a "second presence," meaning that Christ has ascended his heavenly throne. For them, then, the return is exclusively a heavenly reality, in no sense signifying a physical presence of Christ on the earth. As with the Adventists, much is made of the Battle of Armageddon, which is perceived as the worst catastrophe within human history.

Other views of the return may be mentioned very briefly. Christian Science at times equates the Second Coming with the rise of "divine science" in 1866-67. Mormonism teaches that Christ will return before the Millennium and will reign on earth for the thousand years; its doctrine here is not significantly different from that of more "mainstream" Christians. Perhaps most novel is the view of Catholic feminist theologian Mary Daly, who interprets the Second Coming as meaning the rise of feminism in the church: "the Second Coming is not a return of Christ but a new arrival of female presence."

"End-Time" Writers

Hal Lindsey is perhaps the best known of the "students of prophecy" who have written and continue to write about Christ's return. He is familiar to the masses through his book *The Late Great Planet Earth*, as well as several more recent works that explore themes implicit in his early book. An update and summary of *Planet Earth* has been prepared by Lindsey from which we will extract an essence.

Lindsey starts by reminding us that the world is in a desperate situation in almost every respect—morally, economically, religiously. (It is slightly humorous to read statements in Lindsey such as the following: "One scientist recently predicted that by 1980 you will not be able to go on the street without a special breathing apparatus or gas mask." I am writing my comments in late 1984 and, except for a few days after Mount St. Helens erupted, have never needed such appurtenances!) While one may disagree with the radical tone of Lindsey's statements here, and may deplore the unscholarly method of presentation, it is difficult to disagree with some on the main points he makes.

Seven signs of the return are then given. They are:

1. The Jews return to Palestine
2. The Jews possess old Jerusalem
3. The Jews will rebuild the temple in old Jerusalem
4. The "kingdom of the north" (Russia) will attack Israel, "triggering the last war of the world."
5. There will be an Arab confederation led by "the king of the south (Egypt)," but Russia will make a "lightninglike thrust" and conquer all of Africa.
6. An Asian confederacy led by China will be formed, which will march to the banks of the Euphrates, which will be miraculously dried up.
7. Ancient Rome will be revived, a ten-nation confederacy which Lindsey equates with "Modern Europe." The Anti-Christ (or "future Fuehrer") will rule along with the "false prophet," a religious leader. The Common Market will lay the foundation for this revival. The world-ruler will promise peace and economic stability, but at the price of allegiance to himself. The church will become apostate, untrue to its Lord. Before Christ takes up His people, there will be "the greatest time of evangelization ever known here on earth." All this will climax in a seven-year period, including the "Great Tribulation."

Lindsey builds upon the dispensational theology of Dallas Theological Seminary, which in turn bases itself on the work of nineteenth century Bible student J. N. Darby. It should be obvious to the reader that my book assumes a general point-of-view different from that of Lindsey. But this is not to say that we should dismiss him out of hand. Some of his insights are valuable and valid, if one can dissociate them from his methods of presentation.

Tim LaHaye, wide-ranging Christian author whose books are largely in the area of popular psychology and Christian

counseling, has written a book on the Second Coming, *The Beginning of the End*. Like most other "end-time" books, this starts with a discussion of the signs. He accepts the traditional list—false messiahs, wars, and rumors thereof, famine, earthquake—with alleged evidence of the increasing severity of each. He emphasizes that the signs are just the *beginning* of sorrows, and do not of themselves necessarily lead to the end. Particularly interesting is his view that World War I was *the* sign, and others tend to follow from that. One who travels through the British Isles and certain parts of continental Europe sees a great many monuments to the fallen soldiers of that war, testifying to its devastating effect, though this in itself would not necessarily support his thesis.

The "infallible sign" for him is the founding of the modern Jewish state in 1948. Relying largely on the vision of the dry bones in Ezekiel 37 (and surprisingly not on the "fig-tree" passages in the New Testament), he sees the dry bones as coming together in modern Israel. Much is made of the fact that in the 1967 War, Israel regained the temple area and so would be able to rebuild its temple (absolutely essential to Christ's coming, according to LaHaye's school of interpretation). Like Lindsey, LaHaye sees much "prophetic" significance in the modern role of Russia.

One cannot help but be impressed with LaHaye's spirit shown in the writing of his book. He is at every point a Christian evangelist, and is to be commended for it. Also he writes well and shows good breadth of general knowledge. Unfortunately, he does not show similar theological breadth. Typical is his use of the word "prophecy," which he uses almost exclusively in the sense of *fore*-telling, instead of what most of the Christian world understands to be the principal ingredient of prophecy, *forth*-telling, or telling forth God's will. In addition, some of his arguments, such as the rumor that Indiana limestone may be sent to rebuild the temple in Jerusalem, are so devoid of merit as to make one wonder if he can really be serious.

Within the narrow world of his apocalyptic understanding, he does well. But I am sorry that world is not wider.

David Wilkerson, well-known author of *The Cross and the Switchblade*, has in recent years joined the rank of apocalyptic writers. What he says is not uniquely different from the others except in the style of writing. If Lindsey is a stern Amos warning the nations, and LaHaye a gentler Hosea doing the same, Wilkerson is a thundering Nahum, saying, "Woe to the blood city" (country)! It is hard to recall a modern Christian writer whose denunciations are more shrill and whose accusations of America and the world are more pointed than Wilkerson. Many of his criticisms of "The United States of Sodom" are doubtless true, but could apply also to other nations and other times. Also, one is disturbed at his tendency to assume the role of modern prophet to whom God has entrusted visions of the future; can we forget the thousand-plus visions of Ellen White of the Seventh-Day Adventist Church? And one wonders if Wilkerson remembers that "judgment" in the Bible is not necessarily negative, but may connote bringing vindication to the oppressed as much as punishment to the oppressors.

But even this modern Nahum has an ultimate message of comfort: "The bad news is really good news!" Since all these (bad) things must happen before the end, "Christians rejoice because the bad news is a series of signposts clearly marked out on their roadmap to eternity." And a small pastoral word may be worth mentioning. To those who worry that God will keep them through the night, Wilkerson recommends what he well terms "pillow faith." A surprise note of comfort from a most uncomforting writer!

A brief reference to a contemporary "Jesus people" group may be in order. In the magazine *Cornerstone* (Vol. 12, Issue 67) appears a short article on the return. The author, John Trott, deplores the attitude of those who ignore or minimize the event. To do so is to challenge biblical authority itself. Also deplored is the tendency to attach "umpteen tangents" to the

great doctrine, such as the insinuation that certain nefarious groups are carefully orchestrating events to bring in the Antichrist. The recognition of the reality of the coming can have various good consequences, such as a deeper hunger for righteousness and a greater sense of social responsibility. The bottom line is that we are to watch and be ready, recognizing that "God is real, and that He controls history from beginning to end." For those who think of "Jesus People" as some kind of extremists or fanatics, the moderate and reasonable tone of this article should be reassuring.

Our survey would not be complete if we spoke only of *books* dealing with the return. Music is also a potent force. An example is a group that performs what is called "apocalyptic rock." One of their albums having been chosen as an example, many of the songs deal with general Christian themes and only hint at the Second Coming. But one of them, "Ark," deals directly with it. Describing the frantic pounding on the ark door when the flood came, the song says:

> Jesus will come like a thief in the night
> To take all the ones who love him away
> The Body of Christ is the Ark the Lord has given us
> Come and get on board today.

Here we see the primitive—and therefore authentic and dominant—New Testament stress on the unexpectedness of the return, "like a thief in the night." As noted earlier, this is the prevailing New Testament emphasis.

The Author's Choices

One of the most helpful—and even beautiful—treatments of the return is found in a short book, *The Return of Christ*, by Charles R. Erdman, a professor at Princeton Theological Seminary in the earlier twentieth century. Though by now an older discussion of the subject (1922), it was so well done that it is worth considering even now. Erdman begins by pointing out that the doctrine is in many of the greatest hymns, starting with the *Dies Irae*, and in the great creeds as well. An intensely practical belief, it is a motive to "repentance, sobriety, sincerity, watchfulness, patience, fidelity, endurance, hope, love, and to the manifestation of practically every virtue and moral excellence." The ultimate proof of a true doctrinal understanding is for him in "beauty of character and in a growing likeness to Christ." Furthermore, the belief should promote Christian fellowship and "bind believers into a closer union."

As for specifics, he warns against confusing the return with the fall of Jerusalem, Pentecost or one's own death. The events

preceding the coming are wars, tribulation, apostacy and the Antichrist. "The surpreme precedent condition" of His coming, however, is a positive one: *world evangelization* (a point stressed several times). The idea of a "secret rapture" is rejected. His view of the thousand years is that of a modified premillennialist, but emphasis is placed on the unity of the various millennial views, since all agree on: (1) the fact of Christ's return and (2) that it will result in a perfected kingdom of God on earth.

A minor but interesting book on our subject is Louis Berkhof's *Second Coming of Christ*. Like Erdman's book, it is not a recent study; and unlike Erdman it is surprising in that scholars of Berkhof's theological position (strong Calvinism) do not usually write on this theme. This theologian emphasizes the seeming contradiction in a coming that is at one time portrayed as imminent but another as distant; yet both, of course, must be regarded as true. There is no disparity between the "thief in the night" or suddenness theme and the signs, for "the predicted signs are not of such a nature as to designate the exact time of the Lord's return." While not particularly emphasizing the signs, Berkhof sees significance in a possible conjunction of them. Finally, he gives us food for thought in his statement. "We look forward to the *completion* of the one coming of the Messiah." The return as not a second coming but a completion of a coming already begun adds a new dimension to our thought.

One of the finest of recent books (1974) on the return is *The Jesus Hope* by Professor Stephen Travis of St. John's College, Nottingham, England. This Cambridge-educated scholar deals most helpfully with many of the issues that perplex us. Particularly useful is his handling of the "signs of the times." At the Mount of Olives, Jesus' disciples asked him when he would return to satisfy their curiosity as well as to meet their need for psychological security. However, "Jesus did not give them a sign, but a baffling list of signs" that were indicative of the

struggle between good and evil. They were "signs that the end was on its way, but not signs which enable us to work out God's timetable." And they were signs not just of the final days preceding the return, but covered "the whole period from Jesus' resurrection to his final coming." The marks of the last days (that is, of the whole period just referred to) are: false messiahs, with cults as the prime example; world conflict and natural disaster; persecution of his followers; world evangelization; and the fall of Jerusalem as "a prelude to the ultimate showdown." Using the famous D-Day/V-Day analogy, he sees the return as the completion of what was begun at the First Advent: "Christ won the battle *in principle* at his first coming, but the victory will not be *complete* until his return."

C. S. Lewis

"The World's Last Night," an essay by C. S. Lewis, is one of his very few writings concerning the Second Coming. It is also quite basic to my book, which is divided according to three phrases from the essay. It deals chiefly with the grounds of our modern embarrassment relative to the subject. First are the theoretical reasons. One is the possible association, in the public mind, with Albert Schweitzer and his overstress upon the apocalyptic element in Jesus' thought. Lewis is sympathetic, but wisely observes that where an idea has been exaggerated, we should be careful not to overlook it. Another reason for the modern feeling of malaise is Jesus' own admitted ignorance concerning the time of his return. Lewis goes further here than would most conservative writers—including myself—when he says that Jesus "shared, and indeed created" the delusion of the early Christians that Christ would return almost immediately. But the positive side of it is that the willingness of the gospel writers—especially Mark—to record this shows their honesty. Lewis sees all this as a real implication of the

Incarnation: if God was *truly* to become man, and not merely a semblance or appearance of a human being, this necessarily involved (temporary) limitations upon his power (see Phil. 2:5-11, where Paul says Christ "emptied himself" and became man).

Lewis also re-emphasizes a familiar theme in his writings—the "Great Myth" of social evolution or inevitable progress. The doctrine of the return is "deeply uncongenial to the whole evolutionary or developmental character of modern thought." But this does not bother Lewis, who regards this modern evolutionary view as a myth (He is not thinking here only of biological evolution, which he carefully separates from social evolution).

A practical reason for the modern embarrassment is the tendency of believers in the doctrine to set dates. We are players in a great drama, says Lewis, but "we do not and cannot know when the world drama will end." Only the Author knows whether we are in Act I or Act V. Instead of setting dates and letting the concept dominate our lives with fear (or hope), we should rather be sure always to take it into account, in the same way that a person of seventy must not always be thinking of his death, but will take it into account in such matters as planning for the future and making a will. In it all we must be able to give—indeed, to *live*—an answer to John Donne's question, "What if the present were the world's last night?"

Perhaps a fitting conclusion to this appendix is reference to an article in *Time Magazine*, Jan. 8, 1973, entitled, "Is the End Near?" Appearing soon after Christmas, the article asserts that while all Christians celebrate Christ's (first) coming, many are also thinking of His Second Coming. This has been true from the very beginning, when many early Christians believed the event would come in their lifetime or shortly after. Much of the Bible, including parts of the Old Testament, and especially the Book of Revelation, testifies to the importance of this theme. Attention is given to recent popular writers,

especially Lindsey; but Dutch theologian G. C. Berkouwer has the last word: there is no place in the Christian life for calculation of the time of the return, but "the coming salvation can only be awaited in a state of complete preparedness." C. S. Lewis could not have said it better!

Preface to Moody Sermon

This sermon by D. L. Moody, American evangelist of the later nineteenth century, is one to which people of various denominations and theological positions can rally. I am impressed by its reasonableness, its lack of dogmatism and its "centrist" quality: it does not spend time on small details but emphasizes the essentials. If one wishes a similar sermon by a twentieth century theologian, I recommend "When Christ Comes and Comes Again," by Prof. T. F. Torrance.

The Second Coming of Christ.

By D. L. Moody

[Revised]

In 2 Timothy 3:16, Paul declares: "All Scripture is given by inspiration of God, and is profitable for doctrine, for reproof, for instruction in righteousness"; but there are some people who tell us, when we take up prophecy, that it is all very well to be believed, but that there is no use in one trying to understand it; these future events are things that the Church does not agree about, and it is better to let them alone, and deal only with those prophecies which have already been fulfilled. But Paul doesn't talk that way; he says: "All Scripture is . . . profitable for doctrine." If these people are right, he ought to have said, "Some Scripture is profitable; but you can't understand the prophecies, so you had better let them alone." If God didn't mean to have us study the prophecies, he wouldn't have put them into the Bible. Some of them are fulfilled, and he is at work fulfilling the rest, so that if we do not see them all completed in this life, we shall in the world to come.

I don't want to teach anything dogmatically, on my own

authority; but to my mind this precious doctrine—for such I must call it—of the return of the Lord to this earth is taught in the New Testament as clearly as any other doctrine in it; yet I was in the Church fifteen or sixteen years before I ever heard a sermon on it. There is hardly any church that doesn't make a great deal of baptism, but in all of Paul's epistles I believe baptism is only spoken of thirteen times, while it speaks about the return of our Lord fifty times; and yet the Church has had very little to say about it. Now, I can see a reason for this;

THE DEVIL DOES NOT WANT US TO SEE THIS TRUTH,

for nothing would wake up the church so much. The moment a man takes hold of the truth that Jesus Christ is coming back again to receive his followers to himself, this world loses its hold upon him. Gas stocks and water stocks and stocks in banks and railroads are of very much less consequence to him then. His heart is free, and he looks for the blessed appearing of His Lord, who, at His coming, will take him into His blessed Kingdom.

In 2 Peter 1:20, we read: "No prophecy of the Scripture is of any private interpretation." Some people say, "Oh, yes, the prophecies are all well enough for the priests and doctors, but not for the rank and file of the Church." But Peter says, "The prophecy came not by the will of man, but holy men spake as they were moved by the Holy Ghost," and those men are the very ones who tell us of the return of our Lord. Look at Daniel 2:45, where he tells the meaning of that stone which the king saw in his dream, that was cut out of the mountain without hands, and that broke in pieces the iron, the brass, the clay, the silver, and the gold. "The dream is certain, and the interpretation thereof sure," says Daniel. Now, we have seen the fulfillment of that prophecy, all but the closing part of it. The kingdoms of Babylon and Medo-Persia and Greece and Rome have all been broken in pieces, and now it only

remains for this stone, cut out of the mountain without hands, to smite the image and break it in pieces till it becomes like the dust of the summer threshing-floor, and for this stone to become a great mountain and fill the whole earth.

BUT HOW IS HE GOING TO COME?

We are told how he is going to come. When those disciples stood looking up into heaven at the time of His ascension, there appeared two angels, who said unto them (Acts 1:2): "Ye men of Galilee, why stand ye gazing up into heaven? This same Jesus which is taken up from you into heaven shall so come in like manner as you have seen Him go into heaven." How did He go up? He took his flesh and bones up with Him. "Look at me; handle me; a spirit has not flesh and bones as ye see me have." I am the identical one whom they crucified and laid in the grave. Now I am risen from the dead and am going up to heaven. He is gone, say the angels, but He will come again just as He went. An angel was sent to announce His birth of the Virgin; angels sang of his advent in Bethelem; an angel told the women of His resurrection, and two angels told the disciples of His coming again. It is the testimony in all these cases.

I don't know why people should not like to study the Bible, and find out all about this precious doctrine of our Lord's return. Some have gone beyond prophecy, and tried to tell the very day He would come. Perhaps that is one reason why people don't believe this doctrine. He is coming; we know that; but just when He is coming we don't know. Matthew 24:36, settles that. The angels don't know, that is something the Father keeps to Himself. If Christ had said, "I will not come back for 2,000 years," none of his disciples would have begun to watch for Him, until the time was near, but it is

THE PROPER ATTITUDE OF A CHRISTIAN

to be always looking for his Lord's return. So God does not

tell us when He is to come, but Christ tells us to watch. In this same chapter we find that he is to come unexpectedly and suddenly. In the twenty-seventh verse, we have these words, "For as the lightning cometh out of the east and shineth unto the west, even so shall also the coming of the Son of Man be." And again in the forty-fourth verse, "Therefore be ye also ready, for in such an hour as ye think not the Son of man cometh."

Some people say that means death; but the Word of God does not say it means death. Death is our enemy, but our Lord hath the keys of Death; He has conquered death, hell and the grave, and at any moment He may come to set us free from death, and destroy our last enemy for us; so the proper state for a believer in Christ is waiting and watching for our Lord's return.

In the last chapter of John there is a text that

SEEMS TO SETTLE THIS MATTER.

Peter asks the question about John, "Lord, what shall this man do? Jesus said unto him, If I will that he tarry *till I come*, Follow thou me. Then went this saying abroad among the brethren that that disciple *should not die*." They did not think that the coming of the Lord meant death; there was a great difference between these two things in their minds. Christ is the Prince of Life; there is no death where He is; death flees at His coming; dead bodies sprang to life when He touched them or spoke to them. His coming is not death; He is the resurrection and the life; when He sets up His kingdom there is to be no death, but life forevermore.

There is another mistake, as you will find if you read your Bibles carefully. Some people think that at the coming of Christ everything is to be all done up in a few minutes: but I do not so understand it. The first thing He is to do is to take His Church out of the world. He calls the Church His bride, and He says He is going to prepare a place for her. We may judge,

says one, what a glorious place it will be from the length of time He is in preparing it, and when the place is ready He will come and take the Church to Himself.

In the closing verses of the fourth chapter of 1 Thessalonians, Paul says: "If we believe that Jesus died and rose again, even so also them which sleep in Jesus will God bring with Him. . . .We which are alive and remain unto the coming of the Lord shall not prevent them which are asleep. For the Lord Himself shall descend from Heaven with a shout, with the voice of the archangel, and with the trump of God, and the dead in Christ shall rise first. Then we which are alive and remain shall be caught up together with them in the clouds to meet the Lord in the air, and so shall we ever be with the Lord. Wherefore, comfort one another with these words." That is, the comfort of the Church. There was a time when I used to mourn that I should not be alive in the millennium; but now

I EXPECT TO BE IN THE MILLENNIUM.

Dean Alford says—almost everybody bows to him in the matter of interpretation—that he must insist that this coming of Christ to take His Church to Himself in the clouds, is not the same event as His coming to judge the world at the last day. The deliverance of the Church is one thing, judgment is another.

Now, I can't find any place in the Bible where it tells me to wait for signs of the coming of the millennium, as the return of the Jews and such like; but it tells me to look for the coming of the Lord; to watch for it; to be ready at midnight to meet Him, like those five wise virgins. The trump of God may be sounded, for any thing we know, before I finish this sermon,—at any rate we are told that He will come, and at an hour when many look not for Him.

Some of you may shake your heads and say; "Oh, well, that is too deep for the most of us; such things ought not to be said before these young converts; only the very wisest characters, such as the ministers and the professors in the

theological seminaries can understand them." But, my friends, you find that Paul wrote about these things to those young converts among the Thessalonians, and he tells them to comfort one another with these words. Here in the first chapter of 1 Thessalonians, Paul says: "Ye turned to God from idols to serve the living and true God, and to wait for His Son from Heaven whom He raised from the dead, even Jesus which delivered us from the wrath to come." To wait for His Son; that is the true attitude of every child of God. If he is doing that he is ready for the duties of life, ready for God's work; aye, that makes him feel that he is just ready to begin to work for God. Then over in the next chapter (1 Thess. 2:19), he says: "For what is our hope, or joy, or crown of rejoicing? Are not even ye, in the presence of our Lord Jesus Christ, at His coming?" And again, in the third chapter, at the thirteenth verse: "To the end that He may establish your hearts unblamable in holiness before God, even our Father, at the coming of our Lord Jesus Christ with all His Saints." Still again, in the fifth chapter and twenty-third verse: "I *pray God* your whole spirit, and soul, and body, be preserved blameless unto the coming of our Lord Jesus Christ." He has something to say about this same thing in every chapter; indeed, I have thought this Epistle to the Thessalonians might be called the Gospel of Christ's coming again.

There are

THREE GREAT FACTS

foretold in the Word of God. First, that Christ should come; that has been fulfilled. Second, that the Holy Ghost should come; that was fulfilled at Pentecost, and the Church is able to testify to it by its experience of His saving grace. Third, the return of our Lord again from Heaven—for this we are told to watch and wait. "till He come." Look at that account of the last hours of Christ with His disciples. What does Christ say to them? If I go away I will send death after you to bring

you to Me? I will send an angel after you? Not at all. He says:
"I will come again and receive you unto Myself." If my wife
were in a foreign country, and I had a beautiful mansion all
ready for her, she would a good deal rather I should come and
bring her to it than to have me send some one else to bring
her. So the Church is the Lamb's wife. He has prepared a mansion for His bride, and He promises for our joy and comfort
that

HE WILL COME HIMSELF

and bring us to the place He has been all this while preparing.

It is perfectly safe to take the Word of God just as we find
it. If He tells us to watch, then watch! If He tells us to pray,
then pray! If He tell us He will come again, wait for Him!
Let the church bow to the Word of God, rather than try to
find out how these things can be. "Behold, I come quickly,"
said Christ. "Even so come, Lord Jesus," should be the prayer
of the Church.

Take the account of the words of Christ at the communion
table. It seems to me the devil has covered up the most precious
thing about it. "For as often as ye eat this bread and drink
this cup, ye do show forth the Lord's death *till He come.* But
most people seem to think that the Lord's table is the place
for self-examination and repentance, and making good resolu-
tions. Not at all; you spoil it that way; it is to show forth the
Lord's death, and we are to keep it up till He comes.

Some people say, "I believe Christ will come on the other
side of the millennium." Where do you get it? I can't find it.
The Word of God nowhere tells me to watch and wait for the
coming of the millennium, but for the coming of the Lord.
I don't find any place where God says the world is to grow
better and better, and that Christ is to have spiritual reign on
earth of a thousand years. I find that

THE WORLD IS TO GROW WORSE AND WORSE,

and that at length there is going to be a separation. "Two

women grinding at a mill; one taken and the other left. Two men in one bed; one taken and the other left." The Church is to be translated out of the world, and of this we have two examples already, two representatives as we might say in Christ's Kingdom, of what is to be done for all His true believer. Enoch is the representative of the first dispensation, Elijah of the second, and, as a representative of the third dispensation, we have the Savior himself, who is entered into the heavens for us, and became the first fruits of them that slept. We are not to wait for the great white throne judgment, but the glorfied Church is set on the throne with Christ, and to help to judge the world.

Now, some of you think this is a new and strange doctrine, and that they who preach it are speckled birds. But let me tell you that many spiritual men in the pulpits of Great Britain are firm in this faith. Spurgeon preaches it. I have heard Newman Hall says that he knew no reason why Christ might not come before he got through with his sermon. But in certain wealthy and fashionable churches, where they have the form of godliness, but deny the power thereof,—just the state of things which Paul declares shall be in the last days,—this doctrine is not preached or believed. They do not want sinners to cry out in their meeting, "What must I do to be saved?" They want intellectual preachers who will cultivate their taste, brilliant preachers who will rouse their imagination, but they don't want the preaching that has in it the power of the Holy Ghost. We live in the day of

SHAMS IN RELIGION.

The Church is cold and formal; may God wake us up! And I know of no better way to do it than to get the Church to looking for the return of our Lord.

Some people say, "Oh, you will discourage the young converts if you preach that doctrine." Well, my friends, that hasn't been my experience. I have felt like working three times as hard

ever since I came to understand that my Lord was coming back again. I look on this world as a wrecked vessel. God has given me a lifeboat, and said to me, "Moody, save all you can." God will come in judgment to this world, but the children of God don't belong to this world; they are in it, but not of it, like a ship in the water. This world is getting darker and darker; its ruin is coming nearer and nearer; if you have any friends on this wreck unsaved, you had better lose no time in getting them off. But some one will say, "Do you then make the grace of God a failure?" No; grace is not a failure, but man is. The antediluvian world was a failure; the Jewish world was a failure; man has been a failure everywhere, when he has had his own way and been left to himself. Christ will save His Church, but He will save them finally by taking them out of the world. Now, don't take my word for it; look this doctrine up in your Bibles, and, if you find it there, bow down to it, and receive it as the Word of God. Take Matthew 24:50: "The Lord of that servant shall come when he looketh not for him, and in an hour that he is not aware of, and shall cut him asunder, and appoint him his portion with the hypocrites; there shall be weeping and gnashing of teeth." Take 2 Peter, third chapter fourth and fifth verses: "There shall come in the last days scoffers, walking after their own lusts, and saying, Where is the promise of His coming? for since the fathers fell asleep, all things continue as they were from the beginning of the creation." Go out on the streets of this city, and ask men about the return of our Lord, and that is just what they would say: "Ah, yes; the Lord delayeth His coming!"

"Behold, I come quickly," said Christ to John, and the last prayer in the Bible is, "Even so, Lord Jesus, come quickly." Were the early Christians disappointed, then? No; no man is disappointed who obeys the voice of God. The world waited for the first coming of the Lord, waited four thousand years, and then He came. He was here only thirty-three years, and then He went away. But He left us a promise that He would

come again; and, as the world watched and waited for his first coming and did not watch in vain, so now, to them who wait for his appearing, shall He appear a second time unto salvation. Now, let the question go round, "Am I ready to meet the Lord if He comes tonight?" "Be ye also ready, for in such an hour as ye think not the Son of Man cometh."

There is another thought I want to call your attention to, and that is: Christ will

BRING ALL OUR FRIENDS WITH HIM

when He comes. All who have died in the Lord are to be with Him when He descends from His Father's throne (Rev. 3:21) into the air (1 Thess. 4:16-17). A brief interval of time ensues between this meeting of all His saints in the air and His coming with all his saints to execute judgment upon the ungodly, to chain Satan in the bottomless pit for the thousand years, and to establish the millennial reign in great power and glory. "Blessed and holy is he that hath part in the first resurrection; on such the second death has no power, but they shall be priests of God and of Christ, and shall reign with Him a thousand years" (Rev. 20:6). "But the rest of the dead lived not again until the thousand years were past; this is the first resurrection" (verse 5). That looks as if the Church was to reign a thousand years with Christ before the final judgment of the great White Throne, when Satan shall be cast into the Lake of Fire, and there shall be new heavens and a new earth (Rev. 20:1-15; 21:1-5).

Now, I want to give you some texts to study:

When we eat the Lord's supper we shew forth his death, until he comes (1 Cor. 11:26).

We are using our talents, until he comes (Luke 19:13).

We are fighting the good fight of faith, until he comes (1 Tim. 6:12-14).

We are enduring tribulation, until he comes (2 Thess. 1:7).

We are to be patient, until he comes (James 5:8).

We wait for the crown of righteousness, until he comes (2 Tim. 4:8).

We wait for the crown of glory, until he comes (1 Pet. 5-4).

We wait for re-union with departed friends, until he comes (1 Thess. 4:13-18).

We wait for Satan to be bound, until he comes (Rev. 20:3).

Notes

1. William Barclay, *The Mind of St. Paul* (New York: Harper & Row, 1961), p. 163.

2. H. H. Rowley, *The Faith of Israel* (London: SCM Press, 1961), p. 200.

3. G. A. Smith, *Isaiah*, I (New York and London: Harpers, n.d.), pp. 140-41.

4. James Stewart, *A Man in Christ* (New York and London: Harpers, n.d.), p. 132.

5. Ibid., p. 271.

6. William Barclay, *The Mind of St. Paul*, p. 165.

7. C. S. Lewis, *Christian Reflections* (London: Geoffrey Bles, 1967), p. 136.

8. Reinhold Niebuhr, *Leaves from the Notebook of a Tamed Cynic* (Chicago: Willet, Clark and Colby, 1929), p. 91.

9. J. N. D. Kelly, *The Pastoral Epistles* (London: A & C Black, 1963), p. 34.

10. William Barclay, *The Gospel of Mark* (Philadelphia: Westminster, 1956), p. 325.

11. J. H. Jowett, *The Epistles of St. Peter* (London: Hodder & Stoughton, 1905), p. 65.

12. Robert Law, *The Tests of Life* (Edinburgh: T & T Clark, 1909), p. 326.

13. R. H. Mounce, *A Commentary of I & II Peter* (Grand Rapids: Wm. B. Eerdmans, 1982), p. 98.

14. J. H. Jowett, *The Epistles of St. Peter*, p. 335.

15. J. M. P. Sweet, *Revelation* (Philadelphia: Westminster, 1979), p. 281.

16. A. B. Bruce, "Matthew," in *Expositor's Greek Testament*, I (Grand Rapids: Wm. B. Eerdmans, n.d.), pp. 296-97.

17. Louis Berkhof, *The Second Coming of Christ* (Grand Rapids: Wm. B. Eerdmans, 1953), pp. 19-20.

18. T. F. Torrance, *When Christ Comes and Comes Again* (London: Hodder & Stoughton, 1957), p. 21.

19. Stephen Travis, *The Jesus Hope* (Downers Grove: InterVarsity Press, 1976), p. 36.

20. Emil H. Brunner, *The Christian Doctrine of the Church: Faith and Consummation*, trans. by David Cairns and T. H. L. Parker (Philadelphia: Westminister, 1960).

21. K. S. Latourette, *A History of the Expansion of Christianity*, I (New York and London: Harpers, 1937), p. 347.

22. J. Kuizenga, "The Challenge of the Cults," *Theology Today*, April, 1944, p. 35.

23. C. R. Erdman, *The Return of Christ* (New York: George H. Doran, 1922), p. 38.

24. P. Schaff, *The Creeds of Christendom*, III, 4th Edition (New York: Harpers, 1919), p. 756.

25. Ibid., p. 784.

26. H. H. Rowley, *The Relevance of Apocalyptic* (New York: Association Press, 1964), p. 163.

27. Reinhold Niebuhr, *The Nature and Destiny of Man*, II (New York: Scribners, 1946), p. 287.

28. Pierre Teilhard de Chardin, *The Future of Man*, trans. by Norman Denny (New York: Harpers, 1964), p. 308.

29. Emil H. Brunner, *The Christian Doctrine of the Church: Faith and Consummation*, part IV, chapter 8.

30. Albert Schweitzer, *The Mysticism of Paul the Apostle* (London: A and C Black, 1956), p. 5.

31. G. B. Caird, *A Commentary on the Revelation of St. John the Divine* (New York: Harper & Row, 1966), p. 288.

BIBLIOGRAPHY

Archer, Gleason, Feinberg, Paul, and Moo, Douglas, *The Rapture: Pre-, Mid-, or Post-Tribulational?* Grand Rapids: Academie Books; Zondervan, 1984.

Asseng, Rolf E., *When Jesus Comes Again*. Minneapolis: Augsburg, 1984.

Bainton, Roland H., *Yesterday, Today and What Next?* Minneapolis: Augsburg, 1978.

Barclay, William, *The Gospel of Mark*. Philadelphia: Westminster Press, 1956.

Barclay, William, *The Mind of St. Paul*. London: Fontana Books, 1961.

Barkun, Michael, *Disaster and the Millennium*. New Haven: Yale University Press, 1974.

Berkhof, Louis, *The Second Coming of Christ*. Grand Rapids: Wm. B. Eerdmans, 1953.

Boatman, Russel, *What the Bible Says About End Time*. Joplin, Mo.: College Press Pub., 1980.

Bratt, John H., *Final Curtain*. Grand Rapids: Baker Book House, 1978.

Brown, David, *Christ's Second Coming*. Grand Rapids: Baker Book House, 1983.

Brunner, Emil, *The Christian Doctrine of the Church, Faith and Consummation*. Translated by David Cairns and T. H. L. Parker.Philadelphia: Westminster Press, 1960.

Bryant, M. and Dayton, Donald W., eds., *Coming Kingdom: Essays in American Millennialism and Eschatology*. New York: Paragon House, 1984.

Caird, G. B., *A Commentary on the Revelation of St. John the Divine*. New York: Harper and Row, 1966.

Clouse, Robert G., ed., *The Meaning of the Millennium: Four Views*. Downers Grove: InterVarsity Press, 1977.

Erdman, Charles R., *The Return of Christ*. New York: G. Doran, 1922.

Erickson, Millard J., *Contemporary Options in Eschatology*. Grand Rapids: Baker Book House, 1977.

Ewert, David. *And Then Comes the End*. Scottdale, Pa.: Herald Press, 1980.

Feinberg, Charles L., *Millennialism: The Two Major Views*. Chicago: Moody Press, 1980.

Gundry, Robert H., *The Church and the Tribulation*. Grand Rapids: Zondervan, 1973.

Harrison, John F., *The Second Coming: Popular Millenarianism*. New Brunswick: Rutgers University Press, 1979.

Hubbard, David A., *The Second Coming*. Downers Grove: Inter-Varsity Press, 1984.

Jowett, J. H., *The Epistles of St. Peter*. London: Hodder and Stoughton, 1905.

Ladd, George E., *The Blessed Hope*. Grand Rapids: Wm. B. Eerdmans, 1956.

Latourette, K. S., *A History of the Expansion of Christianity*, I. New York and London: Harpers, 1937.

Law, Robert, *The Tests of Life*. Edinburgh: T & T Clark, 1909.

Lewis, C. S., *Christian Reflections*. London: G. Bles, 1967.

Lewis, C. S., *The World's Last Night*. New York and London: Harcourt, Brace Jovanovich, 1952.

Lindsey, Hal, *The Late Great Planet Earth*. Grand Rapids: Zondervan, 1973:

Lindsey, Hal, *The Liberation of Planet Earth*. Grand Rapids: Zondervan, 1974.

Lindsey, Hal, *Satan Is Alive & Well on Planet Earth*. Grand Rapids: Zondervan, 1974.

Martin, Ralph, *The Return of the Lord*. Ann Arbor: Servant Publications, 1983.

Niebuhr, Reinhold, *Leaves from the Notebook of a Tamed Cynic*. Chicago: Willit, Clark and Colby, 1929.

Niebuhr, Reinhold, *The Nature and Destiny of Man*, II. New York: Scribners, 1946.

Pentecost, J. Dwight, *Things to Come*. Grand Rapids: Zondervan, 1958.

Reese, Alexander, *Approaching Advent of Christ*. Grand Rapids: Kregel, 1975.

Robinson, John A., *Jesus and His Coming*. Philadelphia: Westminster Press, 1979.

Rowley, H. H., *The Faith of Israel*. London: SCM Press, 1956.

Rowley, H. H., *The Relevance of Apocalyptic*. New York: Association Press, 1964.

Schaff, P., *The Creeds of Christendom*, III. New York: Harpers, 1919.

Schweitzer, Albert, *The Mysticism of Paul the Apostle*. London: A and C Black, 1956.

Smith, George Adam, *Isaiah*, I. New York and London: Harpers, 1927.

Stewart, J. S., *A Man in Christ*. New York and London: Harpers, n.d.

Sweet, J. P., *Revelation*. Philadelphia: Westminster Press, 1979.

Torrance, Thomas F., *When Christ Comes and Comes Again*. London: Hodder and Stoughton, 1957.

Travis, Stephen, *I Believe in the Second Coming of Jesus*. Grand Rapids: Wm. B. Eerdmans, 1982.

Travis, Stephen, *The Jesus Hope*. Downers Grove: InterVarsity Press, 1976.

Walvoord, John F. and Walvoord, John E., *Armageddon*. Miami: Life Publishers International, 1979.

White, John Wesley, *Arming for Armageddon*. Milford, Mi.: Mott Media, Inc., Publishers, 1983.

Wood, Leon, *The Bible and Future Events*. Grand Rapids: Zondervan, 1973.